THE
B2B SALES
REVOLUTION

How the buying revolution is making
traditional sales techniques ineffective and
what you can do about it.

JOHN O GORMAN   RAY COLLIS

www.theBuyingRevolution.com

ISBN: 978-1-907725-00-5
© John O Gorman & Ray Collis 2010.
All rights reserved.

This publication is designed to provide accurate and authoritative information in regard to the subject matter covered. It is sold with the understanding that neither the author nor the publisher is engaged in rendering legal, accounting, or other professional services. If legal advice, or other expert assistance is required, the services of a competent professional person should be sought.

Published by:
The ASG Group
Sales Consultants
Dublin, Ireland.
www.theASGgroup.com

CONTENTS

Introduction

The Buying Revolution™
THE TRANSFORMATION OF BUYING

PART 2:

The Selling Revolution™

A TRANSFORMATION OF SELLING IS NEEDED

INTRODUCTION:
The B2B Revolution

PRELUDE TO A REVOLUTION

Do you want to know the new rules for buying in organizations, such as Merrill Lynch, Citigroup, HP, Vodafone and Roche? Are you interested in finding out how these rules can help or hinder your sales success? If yes, then this book is for you.

Getting buyers to buy is proving more difficult than at any time for more than a decade. Helping buyers to buy is the greatest challenge facing today's sellers and it is one which this book has been written to address.

Over the following pages the insights of buyers in major organizations worldwide will reveal how buying decisions are now made and, most importantly, **how salespeople can influence them**.

Do You Know What Today's Buyers Want?

We talked to buyers in many of the world's largest companies to find out just how much buying has changed. We wanted to know how the new realities of the market, as well as mounting compliance standards, were impacting on buying decisions.

We were expecting to hear about slashed budgets, changed priorities, stalled purchases and increasingly hard—nosed buyers. However, nothing could have prepared us for the revelation that awaited us. Modern **buying is undergoing a revolution**, yet **the seller is the last to know**. That is until now.

Buying Has Changed

The stories buyers told us about modern buying were both scary and exhilarating. The transformation in how organizations buy is nothing short of a revolution. The changes include more sophisticated buying processes and vastly changed priorities.

Buyers are holding on to their money and sellers' traditional sales techniques, pitches and proposals are no longer enough to get them to buy. To get them to start buying **sellers must help buyers through the strict steps of the buying process and to build a compelling business case.**

We wrote this book because getting buyers to part with their money is more difficult than ever before! As the image on the cover suggests this book is about how we sellers can help buyers to buy.

Sellers Must Adapt To Survive

Sellers, unaware of these changes, are facing an uphill struggle to win new customers or even keep the ones they already have. Indeed, as this book shows, the number one challenge facing sellers is to <u>adapt traditional sales techniques</u>, strategies and skills to cope with the changes in modern buying. Helping sellers achieve this goal is our mission.

USING THIS BOOK

Thank you for picking up this book.

Before you get started, the following chapter will help you understand why reading this book is important and guide you to getting the most from the time you invest in reading it.

To use the language of the modern buyer, this section will help you to arrive at the business rationale or business case in respect of reading through to the end. It will explain all of the following aspects of the book:

- **PROPOSITION**: Why you should read this book.
- **ROI**: How you should measure the success of this book.
- **USPs**: Five things you should know about this book.
- **BENEFITS**: How you will benefit from this book.
- **STRUCTURE**: How this book is structured and how to read it.
- **METHODOLOGY**: The science behind this book.

I. WHY YOU SHOULD READ THIS BOOK

The reason for reading this book is simple. **It will help you to increase or at least maintain your sales success in what is an increasingly demanding B2B marketplace.** How can we so confidently make this assertion? Well, for three reasons:

1. **Because it has helped others.** The ideas, principles and techniques contained in this book are in daily use by hundreds of sellers, as well as buyers. They have proven their worth in the marketplace, enabling sellers to stop the slide in results from using traditional sales and marketing strategies, and boost levels of sales productivity and effectiveness.

   Our extensive analysis and benchmarking of buying practice and selling has enabled the validation of all key aspects of this book.

2. **Because it is written by the very people who make buying decisions** — buyers. After all, who better to advise sellers on how to sell more, than buyers? That makes this book different to just about every other sales book. Indeed, if we are not mistaken, it is the first sales book written by buyers.

3. **Because many sellers are handicapped by an inadequate knowledge of the buying process** in their target accounts. Indeed, a prevailing, over simplistic view of buying is the number one reason for shocks and surprises in respect of sales. It compounds the challenge of predicting what deals will close and when, and results in lost sales on a daily basis.

   Salespeople often complain it is difficult to know what buyers are thinking because they are increasingly playing their hands close to their chest. So this book is a rare insight into what buyers want – an opportunity to listen to customers and prospects reveal how they want to be sold to.

The B2B Revolution Introduction

II. MEASURING THE SUCCESS OF THIS BOOK

Because salespeople are used to being measured on results, we would like you to apply the same principle to this book. That means:

(a) Measuring This Book On Performance

Measure us, as the authors, on how well we have captured, communicated and developed ideas in this book based on all our conversations with buyers and sellers. More to the point, we encourage you to measure this book by the degree to which it can help you in your daily sales activities.

(b) Measuring Yourself On Its Application

We are very much aware that however well written this book is, it is meaningless unless the reader applies its ideas with creativity and determination. Our challenge to you is to measure yourself on how you have applied the ideas and techniques in this book to reach new levels of access, engagement and success in respect of your target buyers.

If, in the unlikely event, it does not help you identify ways to increase your sales success put it aside as it is not for you, at least not at this time.

(c) Setting Targets For Results

Targets are an intrinsic part of selling, as well as buying. With this in mind we would like to make them part of this book. Specifically, we recommend readers target a 3% improvement at each stage of the sales cycle/pipeline — sales leads, sales meetings, sales cycles, sales orders and repeat sales — based on implementing what is in this book. This modest target, which is well within reach of most sales organizations, can have a significant overall impact typically resulting in sales revenue growth of up to 33%.

III. 5 THINGS TO KNOW ABOUT THIS BOOK

As a salesperson you know the importance of having strong unique selling points (USPs). In this respect there are some key things you need to know to understand why this book is important for you to read.

- **This book will change the way you sell.** It has been written to help you improve your sales success using techniques that have been approved by demanding buyers and validated by successful sellers. It will tackle many of your traditional assumptions regarding selling and encourage you to ditch out—dated sales techniques. It will guide you in identifying opportunities for improvement, making changes and taking action – all with the objective of increasing sales productivity and effectiveness in a sustainable manner.

- **This is not just a book; it is a manifesto for a bright new age of selling.** Its pages and paragraphs have not just been written merely to interest the reader, but rather they are intended to be a call to action. They have been written to provoke a rethink of some of the fundamental beliefs that underpin much of selling in today's marketplace. The book is a revolutionary cry on the part of all professional salespeople in the B2B market space.

- **This book is not about traditional selling — it is about helping buyers buy.** With almost 800,000 books on the topic of sales listed by Amazon, another selling book is not what the world needs. The focus of this book is buying. That is how sellers can help buyers to buy. That may sound like a play on words, but it is much more fundamental than that. It is recognition that traditional B2B sales skills and techniques are not enough to swing the modern buying decision.

- **This book was not written by us, but by hundreds of buyers and sellers.** As the authors on the cover we are merely the conduits for the insights of so many others. It is this fact that gives the ideas, tools and techniques contained within their power. They have been applied, validated and proven in the real world of B2B selling.

- **The B2B Revolution is more than a book — it is an online movement.** Readers can visit the web pages of www.BuyerInsights.com to delve deeper into the demands of today's buyers, share their ideas, discuss their challenges and look for answers to questions. There you will find articles, tools, videos and lots more that could not fit within the covers of this book.

IV. HOW YOU WILL BENEFIT FROM THIS BOOK

Here are the benefits that others who have joined The Buying Revolution™ have experienced, and we believe you will experience them too.

1. **Increase sales success and conversion rates.** The objective is to convert more sales leads to sales meetings and buying cycles to sales orders by applying the 41 new rules of selling. As mentioned earlier the benefits you can expect to achieve as a result are in the order of a 33% sales boost.

2. **Ensure a better fit between how you sell and how they buy**. Understand how your customers buy, including the key steps, the information requirements, the internal approval process and so on. Tailor your sales approach to fit these needs, and adopt a more consistent, systematic and repeatable process for selling as a result.

3. **Encounter fewer surprises and setbacks.** With longer sales cycles and the associated rise in costs, the surprise loss of an expected sale is particularly painful. With buyers playing their cards ever closer, it is vital that sellers are better able to understand, read and predict buyers and their actions. It is essential, for example, that they are attuned to the early warning signals that often go unnoticed when a sale is close to collapse.

4. **Give clients a more compelling reason to listen, act and buy**. Discover how to make your solution more compelling, reduce the risk of a stalled buying decision and accelerate the sale. The key is helping the buyer to create a compelling business case around the sale. The number one challenge facing most sellers is to move beyond selling products and services or features and benefits to communicating a compelling business rationale for buying from them. That requires connecting with the buyer's strategy, their exposure to risk, as well as the metrics of their business.

5. **Stand apart from other sellers.** With more sellers chasing fewer buyers the pressure is on price and other sources of competitive advantage. The rise of the RFX or competitive tender compounds this problem. Meanwhile, buyers complain about the sameness of the sales pitches and marketing of competing vendors. The challenge facing today's sellers is to find a new basis for competition — helping the buyer to buy and being seen as a trusted advisor and an expert, not a salesperson.

V. How This Book Is Structured

(a) The Structure Of The Book

As with the buyer—seller relationship this book has two parts. The first part is focused on the buyer and the second on the seller. More specifically Part 1 describes the complex and changing nature of modern buying, while Part 2 describes what sellers must do in order to sell to today's increasingly demanding buyers.

Part 1: The Buying Revolution™

THE BUYING REVOLUTION

Learn how important buying decisions are now being made, including the new demands placed on sellers. Look out for the logo of The Buying Revolution™ in the header of each page in Part 1 – that is the bold letter B with a revolutionary red flag.

Part 2: The Selling Revolution™

THE SALES REVOLUTION

Discover how sellers must transform how they sell – from lead generation to proposal writing – in order to meet changing buyer requirements. You will be guided through Part 2 with another icon to be found in the header of each page – that of a 'red hot', or 'up in flames' letter 'S'.

Over the following pages the insights of buyers in major organizations worldwide will reveal how buying decisions are now made (Part 1) and, most importantly, how salespeople can influence them (Part 2).

(b) How To Read This Book

Here are some tips on getting the most from this book.

- **Treat it more like a workbook than a novel** — some people will read this book from cover to cover, while others will hop about from section to section depending on the particular topic that is of most interest to them at a particular time. The choice is yours, however, we recommend that you don't just read it once and put it aside, as is the case with most books. Use the book as an agenda for action. Keep the book nearby and refer to it regularly. Go back to it repeatedly, each time picking a number of actions to implement.

- **Treat it more like a copybook than a library book** — write on it, underline key parts, make notes, write in actions and turn down the edges. Keep it close to hand — in your briefcase or car. Above all, wear the book out!

- **Treat it like a best seller, not a rare manuscript** — share it, pass it around, give a copy to colleagues. Use it to get conversations going — use it in setting the agenda for change.

- **Oh and most of all — enjoy it!**

VI. THE SCIENCE BEHIND THIS BOOK

We categorize sales wisdom into three distinct categories — the herd of sellers, the vanguard of the profession and, the most important group of all, buyers. We call this the ultimate source of sales wisdom.

Here is an overview of each source and how this book leverages all three:

(a) The Wisdom Of Buyers

We have talked to buyers from some of the world's largest companies — names that include Vodafone, Zurich and Merrill Lynch to mention just a few. They revealed the state of modern buying — the increasingly cautious, rigorous and process—driven approach applied to even relatively small purchases.

They also revealed how decisions are made, how suppliers are chosen and, most importantly of all, how they want to be sold to. This information is now available to managers and sets out key opportunities — some 41 in total — to ensure a better fit between buyer and seller at each stage of the sales cycle.

(b) The Wisdom Of Best Practice Selling

We have reviewed almost one million pages of international best practice case studies, books, whitepapers and articles relating to all aspects of sales. The result is a library of best practice strategies, tools and techniques to inspire managers.

There are numerous articles, checklists and guides available online at www.Buyerinsights.com on all key aspects of selling, from how to increase sales meeting effectiveness to warming up cold calls.

(c) The Wisdom Of The Masses

 Over the past two years we have tracked the sales techniques, tools and strategies employed by over a thousand salespeople in the B2B arena. We have sat in on hundreds of sales presentations and sales pitches. We have reviewed a similar number of sales proposals.

The result is a library of what we call 'common practice' and benchmark data to enable managers to compare and contrast their approach to sales with their peers.

So, with the introduction, background and methodology out of the way – the exposition of modern buying is only a page away. Next is Section 1, the appropriately titled 'Welcome to The Buying Revolution™!'

PART I:

The Buying Revolution™

THE TRANSFORMATION OF BUYING

THE BUYING
REVOLUTION

www.theBuyingRevolution.com

SECTION 1:

The Buying Revolution™

WELCOME TO THE REVOLUTION

This is a time of great turbulence in selling. After a decade of buoyant demand sellers are confronted with the realities of a much changed marketplace. However, the dramatic fluctuations in our economic fortunes that have captured headlines worldwide have masked a set of even more far-reaching changes — a major transformation in terms of how organizations buy.

There was a time when the seller was all powerful, when finding buyers was easy and so too was persuading them. Sellers had the training, the techiques, the processes and the information required to stay one step ahead of the buyer. The buyer was putty in the hands of the slick salesperson.

How things have changed. Buyers have thrown off their chains. They have developed new skills, techniques and processes around buying and now have access to as much if not more information than the salesperson. They now call the shots. They are proving more elusive and more demanding than ever before.

Today's buyer is a powerful force to be dealt with. They won't be out-witted or out-manouvered by a slick salesperson or sales technique. The golden age of buying has arrived, but it finds many sellers unprepared. **As buyers wield their new found confidence and power, sellers are feeling the pain.**

The logo or icon we use to denote The Buying Revolution™ says it all. The buyer – denoted by the bold letter 'B' and the revolutionary red flag - has seized control. In just over a decade buying has been elevated to the level of a science, with today's buyer showing greater skills, confidence and power than ever before. Sellers be warned — The Buying Revolution™ is gathering momentum daily.

BEFORE THE REVOLUTION

THE BUYING REVOLUTION

The sophistication of buying threatens to outstrip that of selling. This book offers **a timely warning not to underestimate the complexity of the modern buyer**. It also provides a blueprint on how to adapt traditional selling to contemporary buying.

A Revolution In Buying Is Underway

Behind closed doors — in boardrooms and executive suites everywhere — a radical shift in buying is underway. Organizations have slashed budgets, turned priorities on their heads and transformed buying into a science. They have learned how to buy in a way that will maximize the success of their business, their projects and their teams.

Furthermore they have invested in the processes, structures and skills to make better decisions, get better value and deliver more successful projects. All this is necessary because **purchasing, previously a bureaucratic order-filling function, is now a strategic source of competitive advantage**.

Proclaiming The Revolution

Accelerated by difficult markets and mounting compliance obligations, modern buying is undergoing a major transformation. Organizations have changed almost every aspect of buying — how decisions are made, why decisions are made and even who makes them. The only problem is sellers have not been told about it. That is until now.

It is time to proclaim The Buying Revolution™ — to let sellers everywhere know that buying has changed and that things will never be the same again. The 10 fundamental ways in which buying has changed are shown overleaf.

Fig. 1.1: Proclaiming The Buying Revolution™ – 10 Changes

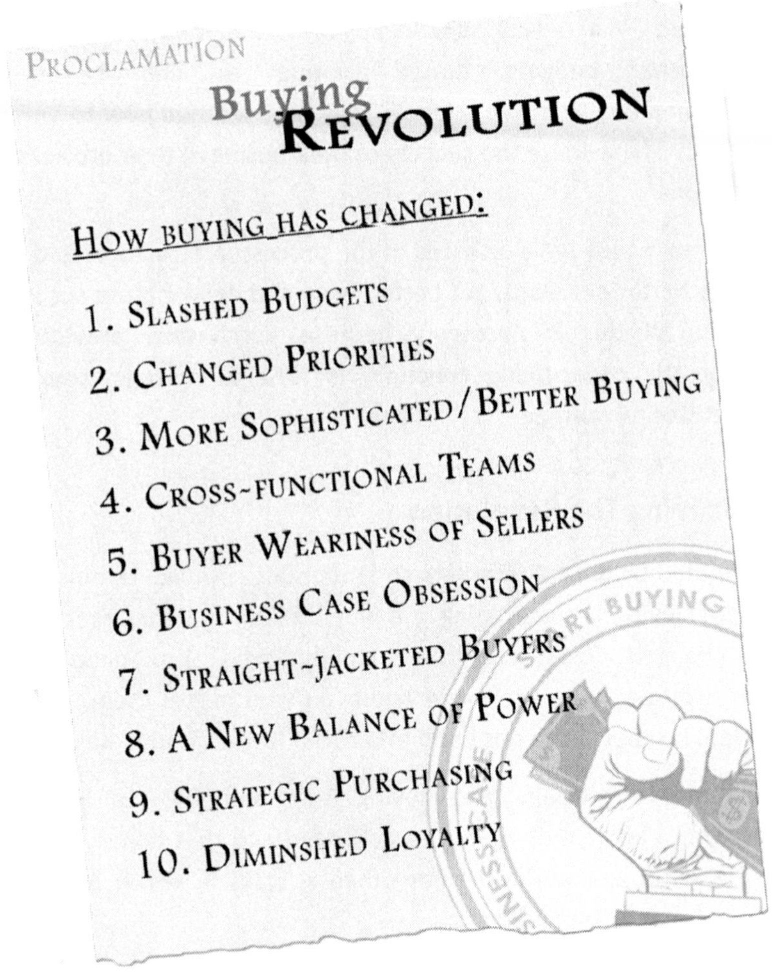

PROCLAMATION

Buying REVOLUTION

HOW BUYING HAS CHANGED:

1. SLASHED BUDGETS

2. CHANGED PRIORITIES

3. MORE SOPHISTICATED/BETTER BUYING

4. CROSS-FUNCTIONAL TEAMS

5. BUYER WEARINESS OF SELLERS

6. BUSINESS CASE OBSESSION

7. STRAIGHT-JACKETED BUYERS

8. A NEW BALANCE OF POWER

9. STRATEGIC PURCHASING

10. DIMINSHED LOYALTY

Even where sellers have been aware of these changes they have been slow to respond. Indeed, most sales organizations are using the same tools, techniques and strategies as they did three, five or even 10 years ago. The result is a continual downward slide in terms of results.

The New Complexity Of Buying

As salespeople we can all too easily underestimate the complexity of buyers and buying. For example, when asked to describe their customer's buying process and, in particular the number of people or steps involved, the answers given by sales professionals are at least out by a factor of two or three.

That is because **the map of how organizations buy is very much out of date**. This has a great number of consequences, including the fact we often unwittingly end up selling the wrong things, in the wrong way to the wrong people.

Changing The Map

Here is a very important parable of modern buying. When you grasp its message you will have mastered one of the key principles of success in the age of the buying revolution.

There is somewhere you need to be and you are under time pressure to get there. You have been handed a map by which to navigate your journey — so you pack your bag and set off with speed, stamina and determination.

The only problem is that the map is not what it purports to be. You want to find your way around London from Piccadilly to Mayfair, but your map is showing Times Square, Central Park and Fifth Avenue. Although the map is labeled correctly it is actually of another city and country. However, because everybody seems to be using the same map you are reluctant to cast it aside.

Instead you re-double your efforts and renew your determination, but **the map keeps sending you in the wrong direction**. Surprises, setbacks and disappointments inevitably result.

However, no matter how much harder you try, your extra effort can only have a limited impact. That is <u>until you change the map that is setting you astray</u>.

The journey is the sale and the erroneous map is our commonly held view of how

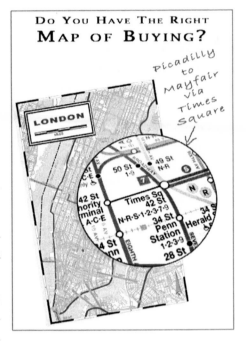

organizations buy. The moral of the story is new sales skills, techniques and strategies can only have limited success until sellers correct the map of how their customers and prospects buy. This is at the core of all the chapters of The Buying Revolution™.

This book has been written to provide you with an accurate and up-to-date map of modern buying. As a result it will help you arrive more confidently at your destination — the sale.

Your New Map Of Modern Buying

Few sellers have ever been shown an actual map of the corporate buying process. We are going to remedy this deficiency immediately because it unquestionably hinders their success.

So, what does a modern buying decision look like? Well, below is a map of the buying process for major IT projects in a *Fortune 1000* organization.

When it comes to the sophistication of modern buying, seeing is believing. The *Fortune 1000* buying process shown here is a wakeup call for most sellers.

Fig. 1.2: A Typical *Fortune 1000* Buying Process

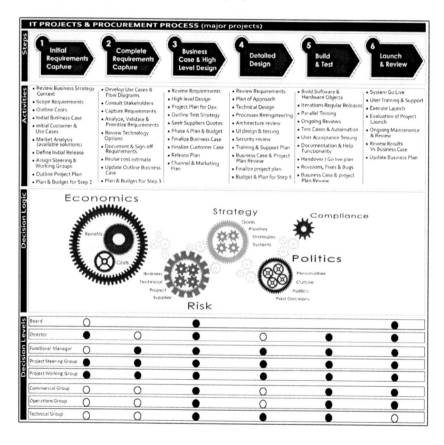

Don't worry if you are not selling IT, or if you are not selling to *Fortune 1000* companies. The principles that the model demonstrates are increasingly reflective of all customers and prospects. The bottom line is most buyers are getting more sophisticated at buying. The model we are set to explore will prepare you for selling to any customer.

Standing back from the detail of the steps and the people involved, the first thing that strikes the salesperson on seeing this process **is just how structured and sophisticated the big company approach to buying is**. It serves notice that buying has been elevated to a science. The problem is that when the science of complex buying meets the traditional art of selling there are likely to be problems.

The picture of modern buying is complicated, perhaps even scary. However, the implications of the changed nature of organizational buying, while dramatic, will vary from seller to seller. For some, in particular those reading this book, it represents an important opportunity. For others it poses a significant threat.

Knowledge is power and by the close of this section any initial anxiety regarding the hidden sophistication of modern buying will give way to a sense of **empowerment, as well as a greater sense of confidence and control**. This will happen as we deconstruct the buying process on three levels as shown in the diagram overleaf.

Fig. 1.3: The Three Levels of The *Fortune 1000* Buying Process

Section 3

How?

Section 4

Why?

Section 5

Who?

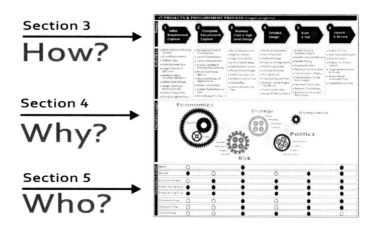

In adopting this structure we examine The Buying Revolution™ on the three levels shown above. That is the how, why and who of the buying decision —more specifically the buying process, the business case and the buying team in turn. To round this off we have added a fourth section aimed at debunking some myths that are inconsistent with the new order of buying.

Structure And Overview Of Part One

So, let's not waste any time in our voyage through the complexities of modern buying and quickly arrive at the implications for all of us involved in sales and marketing. We will do this by deconstructing the typical buying decision to understand the fundamental DNA of modern buying as follows:

BUYING PROCESS
REVOLUTION

S.2: The Buying Process Revolution

<u>HOW</u> THE DECISION IS

MADE

In Section 2 we will examine how modern buying decisions are made, including the rules that must be followed. We will challenge the salesperson to put the buying process ahead of idealized notions of the sales process. You will note the icon used will change when we are talking about the Buying Process to include a process diagram on the red flag.

BUSINESS CASE
REVOLUTION

S.3: The Business Case Revolution

<u>WHY</u> THE DECISION IS

<u>MADE</u>

In Section 3 we will see purchases for as little as $20,000 now typically require a business case. We will examine what the business case contains, and challenge the salesperson to ditch features and benefits selling in favor of influencing the business case. The icon used when we are talking about the Business Case will include a bar chart on the red flag.

S.4: The Buying Team Revolution

WHO MAKES THE DECISION

The center of control for buying has changed, which can result in the salesperson talking to the wrong people. In Section 4 we challenge salespeople to sell higher and wider. The icon used in respect of the Business Team will include an organizational chart on the red flag.

S.5: The Ideological Revolution

EXPLODING SALES MYTHS

In the concluding section, Section 5 *A Revolution in Thinking* we will examine the implications for these changes in terms of commonly held myths about selling. This time the red flag in the icon will include a myth busting symbol.

The icons shown above will help you navigate this book — they are shown on the top right of each page to denote the particular aspect of the revolution being examined. Visually the layout of Part 1 can be seen from the diagram presented overleaf.

Fig. 1.4: The Structure of Part 1

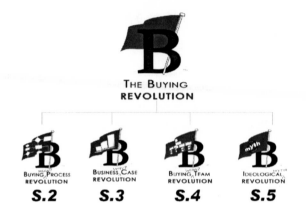

Let's Get Started

Are you ready to unlock the secrets of modern buying and their implications for your sales approach? Then jump straight into the next chapter in which buyers reveal the new basis upon which major purchase decisions are made. Let's get started by discovering what we call *The Buying Process Revolution*.

BUYING PROCESS
HOW?
REVOLUTION

SECTION 2:

The Buying Process Revolution

HOW TODAY'S BUYERS BUY

Organizational buying, once ad hoc and unstructured, has become highly sophisticated and process-driven. Although salespeople have noticed some changes, they often underestimate just how sophisticated buying has now become.

In this section many salespeople will come face-to-face for the very first time with the full complexity of buying — in the form of a *Fortune 1000* buying process. That includes the new steps, activities and people involved, as well as the many implications that result.

What Does Modern Buying Look Like?

'Great idea, let's do it!' is rarely heard from today's buyers. The best sellers can hope for is, 'Let's get a multi-disciplinary team together to develop the business case, then in 4 to 8 months we can decide if it is worth doing.'

When it comes to how organizations buy there is a sophisticated process, which is often very structured and rigid. It is a **scientific process for the allocation of scarce organizational resources** between competing projects or purchases.

To see just how sophisticated today's buying decisions are, we will take an archetype *Fortune 1000* buying process and lay it bare. We will do this at two levels: the <u>STEPS</u> in the buying decision and the <u>ACTIONS</u> at each step.

Fig. **2.1** Examining the Buying Process on Two Levels

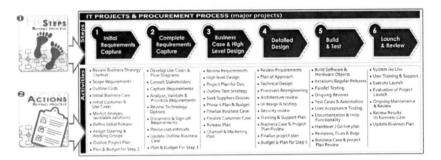

This map of how organizations buy is presented in its full size overleaf.

Fig 2.2 The *Fortune 1000* Buying Process in Detail

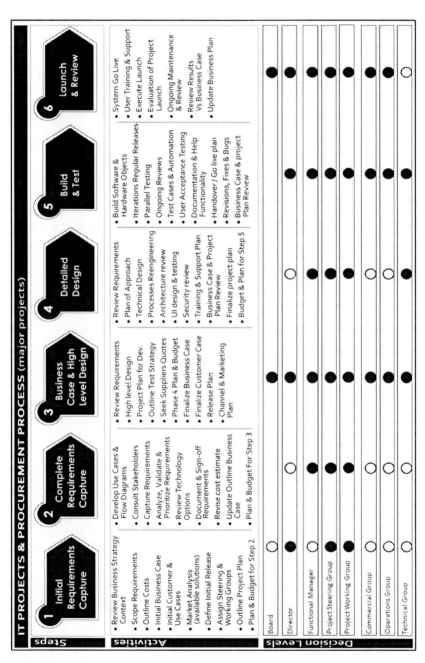

The <u>STEPS</u> Of The Buying Process

In our *Fortune 1000* example managers must follow six key steps to gain purchasing approval. These logical and self-explanatory steps, ranging from Initial Requirements Capture to Launch and Review are shown below.

Fig. 2.3 The 6 Steps of the Buying Process

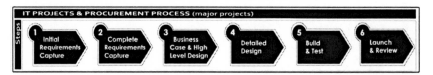

These steps can take place over anything from three months to two years, and are likely to involve dozens of people along the way. Clearly making the right buying decision is not going to be left to the discretion of the buyer-manager, and it is definitively not going to be unduly influenced by the salesperson.

Interpreting the Steps

Looking at this diagram immediately sets sellers thinking about the steps in their own customers' buying process. Our model makes this easy - at a high level it is very easy to overlay onto how any customer is likely to buy. To see this we will re-label the diagram as shown in the diagram overleaf.

The B2B Revolution   Section 2

Overlaying labels such as 'needs analysis' and 'define solution' on the six steps of our *Fortune 1000* model demonstrates the universality of that buying process.

Fig. 2.4: Re-labeling the Buying Process

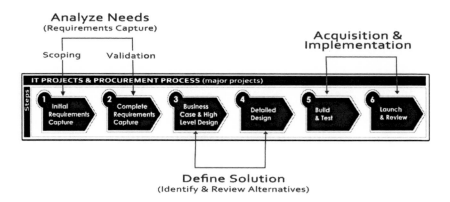

All our customers are likely to progress through the generic stages of needs analysis, solution definition and acquisition, or implementation. However, regardless of whatever labels are used, the implications of such a step-wise approach to buying are what matters most. So, let us examine them now.

Understanding the Implications

As we will see it is the buying process that now dictates the pace of buying, as well as selling. The process ensures decisions are not rushed, but made in a careful and step-wise manner. For the buying organization this should mean better buying decisions, but for the salesperson more steps means more costly and unpredictable sales cycles.

It sounds obvious, but what happens with respect to the purchase decision depends on the step in the process the buyer is actually at. As we will see, the issues, the priorities, the people involved and so on vary from step to step. It follows therefore that the **salesperson must know where the buyer is and adjust their sales approach accordingly**. For example, buyers at Step 1 should be sold to differently than those at Step 3.

When Does The Process Begin Or End?

Most salespeople know that sales cycles are much longer than they used to be. But, if sales cycles are long, then buying cycles are even longer. As our model buying process shows today's buying decisions start earlier and finish later.

The Conception Of The Purchase

The genesis of the purchase is Step 1, the exploratory Initial Requirements Capture stage shown overleaf. This is the purchase decision as an embryo, the result of a non-committal 'let's explore if this is worth exploring' decision.

This is a tentative first pass of the project in terms of the business case, strategic fit and requirements. The outcome at this stage will determine if **the project or purchase merits progressing** to a more detailed and more costly examination.

Fig. 2.5: The Start of the buying Process

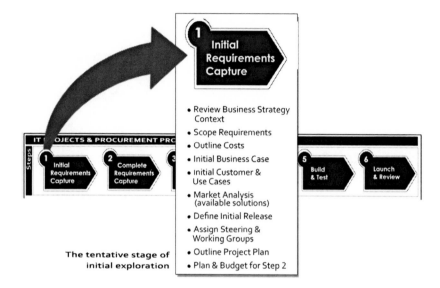

As we will discuss later, the early stages of the buying process will involve little, if any contact with sellers.

The Conclusion Of The Buying Process

The model buying process shows that the process continues to the point of delivery and beyond (Step 6: Launch and Review).

Fig. 2.6: The Last Step of the Buying Process

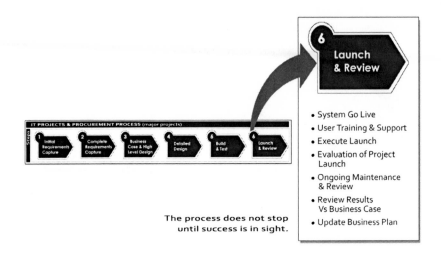

For buyers the process only ends when the strategic goals underlying the purchase have been satisfied. It is **a cradle-to-grave process that includes implementation, management and review**.

The sixth step represents an essential feedback and correction loop for senior executives that ensures what is promised by means of the business case, as well as the seller's proposal, is delivered. It also ensures that buyers get better and better at buying, learning from past mistakes and becoming increasingly accountable for the results that are achieved.

If the seller is not present at the conception of the buying process there is a double danger — that they won't be present at the conclusion either. This happens because sellers often **mistake the purchase order as the finishing line**. For example:

- Once the order is signed the salesperson is under pressure to move on to close the next deal. In the narrow pursuit of the purchase order sellers can fail to recognize that the buying decision is a far longer and more complex process than they realize.
- As many suppliers are learning to their cost projects and purchases can be abruptly terminated post signing. It is not over until the final payment is received and with claw-back provisions often in place, perhaps not even then.
- Winning the first sale requires making promises, while winning the next sale (and indeed the customer) requires that promises made are kept – something that we will see in The Sales Revolution™ cannot be taken for granted.

The Seller In The Middle

So far you are probably thinking this **buying process is all about the buyer** as there has been no mention of the seller yet. Well, now that we have looked at the conception and the conclusion of the Six Step Buying Process, and before we start to examine all the detail that is involved, let us pinpoint the entrance of the seller into the process.

As the diagram overleaf shows the first direct reference to sellers takes place in Step 3 and is shown in the diagram as 'seek supplier quotes'. The fact that this occurs at such a late stage — just before the halfway mark of the process — and is worded in such minimalist terms is a cause of surprise for many.

Fig. 2.7: Looking for the Seller in the Buying Process

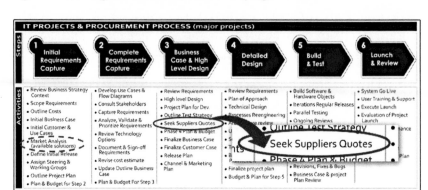

Concerned at what seems to be the **marginalization of the role of the salesperson**, sellers typically ask, 'Is that the earliest reference to suppliers?' Well it is, apart from the Initial Requirements Capture in Step 1 where the review of available solutions in the marketplace takes place — a step that is called 'market analysis' as highlighted by a dotted circle in the diagram above. This step, however, is often conducted without any direct contact with salespeople. This lack of involvement can be attributed to the increased accessibility of information via analysts and other sources. However, there is another factor also at play.

Buyers are increasingly setting the rules of engagement, defining what contact between buyer and seller is appropriate, even permissible, at each stage of the buying process. Little wonder sellers complain that they are being left waiting in the hallway, while the buying decision is made behind closed doors.

The B2B Revolution Section 2

A Step-By-Step Progression Through The Buying Process

Each progressive step brings the purchase one step closer to reality, with the commitment being made gradually over many months. Thus, the purchase decision is not simply a matter of one big YES or NO decision. Rather it is the culmination of a series of YES or NO decisions at each stage of the buying decision. For example:

- 'YES' it is worth doing an initial business case and requirements capture (Step 1).
- 'YES' the initial business case and requirements capture merit further examination — move to complete requirements capture (Step 2).
- 'YES' the detailed business case is compelling (Step 3).
- 'YES' the high-level design is feasible (Step 4) and so on.

At the end of each stage a plan and budget is set out for the next stage and it is on this basis that a decision will be made as to whether the project will progress further.

Fig. 2.8:   The Stop-Go Nature of Buying Decisions

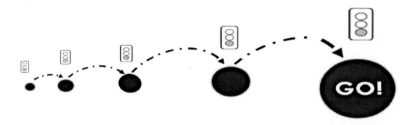

The incremental nature of the buying decision complicates things greatly for the seller. It means that one YES is not enough and that the 'sure thing' sale can be derailed at any stage.

A Step-By-Step Commitment To The Buying Decision

In respect of the complex sale there are no quick wins as the purchase decision is made one step at a time. The implication is that neither the buyer, nor the salesperson can skip a step.

The buying process entails a step-wise progression in terms of commitment until the point where the ultimate spend decision must be sanctioned.

2.9 The Commitment to the Purchase is Step-Wise

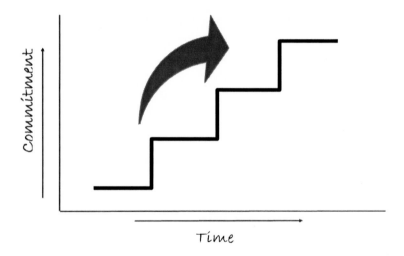

For sellers this step-wise process of commitment has profound implications. The seller must understand the degree of commitment that is possible at any stage of the buying process. It means that **the 'Always Be Closing' mantra does not fit the complex sale.** The salesperson's objective should be to progress to the next stage, rather than to close the sale.

The reality is for every project that successfully navigates the buying process, many more will not. As increasing rigor is applied at each successive stage, more projects will be 'killed off'. In an organizational context, **it is the application of the Darwinian principle** — the means by which budget-strapped organizations seek to ensure the optimal allocation of resources between competing projects. This is important for the seller who often narrowly views another supplier as the only source of competition.

The reality of modern buying is that another competing project represents the greatest threat to winning the purchase order.

Now that we have examined the steps of the buying process let us take a closer look at the detail of the activities taking place at each step.

The <u>ACTIONS</u> Of The Buying Process

So, we have examined the key steps of the buying process. But, within each step, how much discretion remains in the hands of the manager-buyer? Is the buying process a flexible blueprint or a rigid rulebook?

The *Fortune 1000* buying process we have highlighted is highly prescriptive, something that is increasingly common. It clearly mandates what it considers to be 'the science of buying'. This is evident from the list shown overleaf of the actions to be completed for each step. These actions are mandatory, not optional.

Fig. 2.10: The Mandatory Actions At Each Step

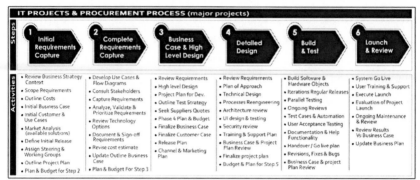

For a larger version of this diagram, see page 17.

Buying in large organizations is the equivalent of painting by numbers, with each step clearly prescribed and little left to chance. As the diagram above shows the process of the *Fortune 1000* organization outlines a total of 59 key activities across the various steps. For sellers impatient with the progress of a sale it is worth noting there are approximately 10 activities to be completed in each of the six steps of the process.

Managers have to complete each step as required thus ensuring a standard approach to buying is adopted organization wide. But as the demands of the buying process grow the key question is: '**How can the seller help the buyer successfully navigate the increasingly demanding requirements of the buying process?**'

Well, before answering this question let us draw some conclusions about the nature of the tasks set out in the buying process model. In particular what it indicates about the nature and sophistication of modern buying.

1. **The process is a cerebral one.** In our example, the terms 'plan' and 'planning' are referred to in 13 places throughout the process. Indeed the process is best described as a planning process. Clearly the decision is not going to be rushed, nor is it likely to be one where the vendor's information is taken at face value. The challenge for the salesperson is to be a part of that planning process.

Fig. 2.11: References to 'Plan' or 'Planning' in the Buying Model

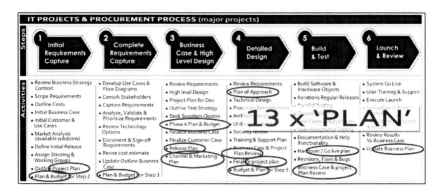

2. **Business logic drives the process.** One of the most consistent themes of the buying process is the 'business case'. As highlighted in the diagram overleaf it is to be found in all six stages of the process examined here. Vendors take note — the terms sales proposal, presentation or pitch do not feature at all. As we will see in Section 3: The Why of the Buying Decision, nothing short of a compelling business case will be required to ensure the purchase gets sanctioned.

Fig. 2.12: References to the 'Business Case' in the Buying Model

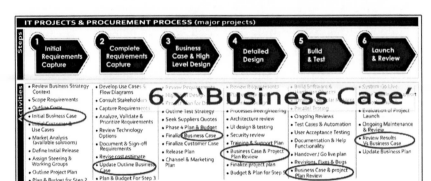

3. **The information requirements of the process are significant.** Each step requires data to be gathered — from the 'market analysis of available solutions' in Step 1 to the 'review of results against the business case' set out in Step 6. It is clear that marketing blurb is going to be of little value to buyers. Sellers must provide information that is expert, valid and useful.

4. **The tasks are very much action oriented** using verbs such as 'outline', 'assign', 'finalize' and so on. Actions are highly practical, with requirements to 'analyze, validate and prioritize requirements' or 'develop use case and flow diagrams'. Buyers are clearly being told what they must do and little is being left to chance.

The implication is the seller's idealized notion of the sales process must flex to the realities of the buying process. The salesperson's new role is to help the buyer navigate the increasingly demanding requirements of their internal processes.

5. **Most of the tasks are centered on producing outputs.** For example, an initial business case is the output of Step 1. The process is evidence-based and highly documented. Typically there is a template/corporate standard for the key outputs of each stage. So, while seller's proposals take a variety of formats, the business case prepared by the buyer is likely to follow a well-defined and consistent standard.

6. **A high level of self-reliance is evident**. For example, buyers are defining their requirements (Steps 1 and 2), defining the solution (Steps 3 and 4) and building the business case (Steps 1 and 3) without recourse to sellers. One might even suspect that the project when defined might be offered to internal resources for completion, as well as to external suppliers.

   Herein lies a major challenge: With the buyer doing much of the work traditionally undertaken by the seller, just where does the salesperson fit in? Finding a way to add value to the buyer's process is absolutely critical.

7. **The buying process is in many ways akin to an internal sales process**. As projects and purchases compete for scarce organizational resources, managers must get buy-in to their projects from all the various stakeholders. This is evident from the 'initial use and customer cases' defined in Step 1 to the 'user acceptance testing' in Step 5.

   In this respect, the seller's job has transitioned from selling to the buyer to helping the buyer sell. Meanwhile, the greater degree of consultation and consensus inherent in modern buying makes the sale slower and more unpredictable.

The seven characteristics of the buying process that we have just described have major implications for the salesperson and the sales approach. This is something that we will discuss as we progress through the remainder of the book.

Applying Buying Process Principles

Having examined the HOW of the buying decision — that is the steps, as well as the activities involved in a real world buying process — we would recommend that you apply it to your key pipeline opportunities. To do this we have provided a checklist overleaf. By doing this exercise your attention is likely to be drawn to some key opportunities to improve the chances of winning the sale. The checklist can also be applied to lost deals, to help you better understand and indeed learn from what went wrong.

In the following chapters we will develop upon our new understanding of the buying process as follows:

- In the next section we will examine the decision-making logic involved in the process (**Section 3: The Business Case Revolution**).
- In **Section 4: The Buying Team Revolution** we will explore the new buying team.
- In **Section 5: The Ideological Revolution** we will use our new understanding of modern buying to explode many of the erroneous myths that are traditionally associated with selling.

How well do you know the buying process involved in your major sales opportunities? To find out apply the following questions to your sales opportunities.

BUYING PROCESS: HOW the decision is going to be made:

BUYING A PROCESS
REVOLUTION

CHECKLIST

	I am Sure	I am Not Sure	ACTIONS
1. What is the buying process?	☐	☐	
2. How rigid, structured, or sophisticated is it?	☐	☐	
3. What are the key steps?	☐	☐	
4. What are the key review/sign-off points?	☐	☐	
5. How long will it take?	☐	☐	
6. What stage in the buying process is the purchase at?	☐	☐	
• Have requirements been defined?			
• Has a business case been created?			
• Has a budget been allocated?			
• Is there a shortlist of vendors? How many? What criterion?			
7. What documentation is required by the buying unit?	☐		

Rate out of 10 Your Buying Proces Knowledge

_____

How well do you feel the buying process has been facilitated by your sales approach: (Out of 10)

_____

The Buying Process Revolution — Summary

Organizations are making slower and, in many cases, fewer buying decisions. But these decisions are being more carefully made, with greater consideration and planning than ever before.

BUYING PROCESS
REVOLUTION

It seems inevitable that all this will lead to better buying decisions or at least decisions that reflect more closely organizational priorities and objectives. However, it also means longer and more complex sales cycles. Here are just some of the implications for the salesperson:

- Sellers must support buyers through their prescribed buying process, even if that does not fit with the seller's idealized sales process.
- Vendors must understand the business decisions behind buying decisions.
- Sellers must be careful not to usurp the buying process by attempting to fast-track access to information and stakeholders, or by closing prematurely.
- Vendors need to reassess the drive for a consistent and repeatable sales process across their sales teams. Trying to corral buyers through the seller's way of selling is likely to encounter resistance.
- The way organizations sell must reflect the stage of the buying process that the buyer is at. In particular, it must recognize that the buying process starts earlier and finishes later than ever before.

BUSINESS CASE
REVOLUTION

SECTION 3:

The Business Case Revolution

WHY BUYERS BUY

Why do buyers do what they do? Why do they choose one supplier over another and choose some projects to be scrapped, while others are advanced? These are questions that understandably intrigue salespeople.

Buyers tend to reveal little, leaving many salespeople complaining that they don't know what buyers are thinking. They may even complain buyers say one thing and then do another. However, in the case of major buying decisions there is – as this section will demonstrate - in reality little mystery.

Sellers need to understand what the buyer is thinking, as only then can they truly shape the buying decision. So, just what is on a buyer's mind as the seller delivers a pitch or proposal? Well, we asked buyers to reveal what they are looking for in sellers, the factors involved in making decisions and the rationale behind allowing some projects proceed while many others are scrapped. They revealed to us the logic behind their buying decisions.

What Is The Buyer Thinking?

The buying process examined in Section 2 clearly demonstrates that the buying decision is carefully made – it involves much information gathering, analysis and planning. That in itself reveals much about what buyers are thinking.

So, why do buyers chose one supplier, over another, for example? Well, one thing for sure is that it is less determined by the persuasiveness and influence of the salesperson than at any time in the past. They are making their own minds up.

Indeed, **the rationale behind modern buying decisions is clearer and more focused than ever before.** Our many conversations with buyers pointed to how remarkably consistent buyers are in terms of how they buy. Every purchase they make is evaluated in terms of 5 key factors:

1. Economics.
2. Strategy.
3. Politics.
4. Risk.
5. Compliance.

There are other factors, such as technology or supplier choice, however, all of these factors fit neatly into one of the above five buyer preoccupations.

Buyer Logic Examined

Clearly one of the key trends in respect of organizational buying is the movement towards **the application of business logic to business decisions**. It is clear that features and benefits will not swing the big sale, forcing the seller to address the key economic, strategic and political issues if the purchase is to be sanctioned.

Fig. 3.1: The Logic of the Buying Decision

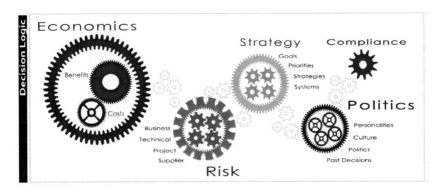

There is certainly still a role for emotion and politics in complex buying. However, the increasingly structured steps of the buying process, as well as the process of sign-off and approval, have had the effect of putting **business logic at the core of the buying decision**. Remember, in the *Fortune 1000* buying process model we featured in Section 2 the terms 'planning' and 'business case' were mentioned almost 20 times.

The Buying Decision

The sales professionals succeeding in today's business environment truly **understand the combination of economics and strategy** at the center of modern buying decisions. There is no alternative.

If salespeople attempt to woo buyers with anything less than solid business logic, say for example by listing the features and benefits, their luck is bound to fail them. The logic of the business case now dictates every element of the buying process, from initial need recognition through to buyer selection and onwards.

What Is The Business Case?

One of the most powerful realizations for sellers is that when it comes to the complex sale **there are no buying decisions, only business decisions**. The implication is that buying decisions which in the past focused on the what, where, when and how, are now purely concerned with the 'why?' Peel back the layers of any important buying decision and you will find the business case at the core.

Fig. 3.2: The Business Case is at the Core of The Buying Decision

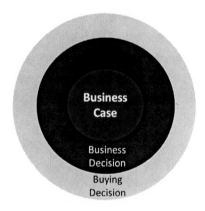

For those who have studied business, almost at any level, business logic and the business case should be something very familiar. It is the application of business 101 principles — in other words business decisions should be made to maximize (long-term) economic return.

Managers have a responsibility to their shareholders — to grow profits, revenue and asset values. This requires the application of hard-nosed business logic to <u>all</u> business decisions, including those relating to major purchases. It also requires **decision making that is based on good information, analysis and planning**.

The New Battleground For Sellers

The business case is the new battleground for buyer and seller alike:

- When purchases get stalled or scrapped it is because the business case is not strong enough.
- When a seller loses a sale it is because their proposal fails to demonstrate how their company is essential to the buyer's business case.
- When projects struggle and fail to deliver the expected results, it is because of problems in the transition from business case to business reality.

Buyers tell us that the business case is more important than the skill of the salesperson, the reputation of the supplier, the quality of the sales proposal, the sophistication of the technology or just about anything else. After all **unless there is a compelling business case the purchase will not proceed**.

Salespeople Grapple With The Business Case

Despite its importance, most salespeople struggle with the business case. First, there is confusion about what the business case is and what it should contain. Then there is anxiety about how the seller can get to see the business case, not to mention how they can actually influence it. These factors have **greatly diminished the influence the salesperson** has on how buying decisions are made.

The fundamental importance of business logic or the business case is the iron law of buying. We call it a law because it is fixed and immutable. Its existence does not depend on the seller understanding the need for a business case, or what it should contain. It does not depend on the seller seeing the business case, or even influencing it. The business case is at the center of big buying, whether the salesperson likes it or not.

The challenge for the salesperson is to replace the terms competitive advantage, features and benefits with the language of the business case. This section has been written with this in mind.

The Business Case Examined

Before managers or departments can get 'the green light' for a major purchase they must answer in a compelling way the following questions:

- Why fund this expenditure?
- Why now?
- Why support this project instead of another?

These questions can only be answered by reference to the business case.

In a turbulent marketplace, with greater uncertainty, heightened sensitivity to risk and pressure on budgets, **managers need a compelling reason to commit to new projects and expenditures**. That reason is communicated by means of the business case.

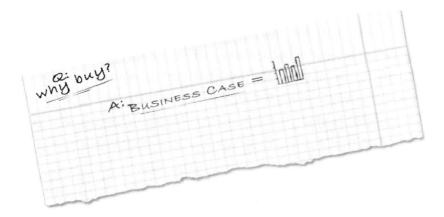

The business case can take many forms, but at its core is one key question — how will this purchase help the organization (department/unit) succeed?

BUYER INSIGHT

'Most buyers say they have a big picture view that sellers cannot see. That is how the purchase fits with their organization's priorities, strategies and goals. In other words they are looking beyond the purchase to the results.'

It clearly outlines the value equation of the proposed purchase that reflects not only costs, benefits and risk, but also how the project will contribute to the achievement of broader organizational goals and strategies. This is the new reality of the business case sale.

Let us explore what the business case entails and how it represents a radical departure for both buyer and seller. First, let us be clear as to what is and is not a business case.

The Cost-Benefit Equation

Most sellers fail to give the business case the focus and attention it now demands. That is because the solution being sold, what it does and how it does it, is the stuff of traditional sales presentations, not the business case. **The business case is concerned only with results and outcomes**, or more precisely benefits minus costs and consequences.

The number one job of the business case is to **calculate the business impact and results of the proposed purchase**. At the highest level that means the critical elements are the top line, the bottom line, and so on. We refer to this as 'CEO proofing the business case' — making it appeal to issues of concern to the CEO. The metrics will vary depending on whether it is the CFO, the CEO, or the COO, however a business case has to be quantified.

For sellers this can be a challenge because they often struggle to move beyond adjective-laden benefit statements to the cold science of numbers. This is something that we will discuss in Part 2: The Sales Revolution™ Section 4.

Considerations Of Risk

The business case requires much more than a cost-benefit analysis — that is too simplistic for complex business decisions. For example, a more in-depth analysis would highlight that while the payback from project A might be twice that of project B, this benefit may be negated when higher levels of risk are considered. Managers are increasingly concerned with risk and for good reason. That is the risk the desired results will not be achieved or that other unwanted consequences will arise.

For buyers this is the era of playing it safe. The appetite for risk has diminished greatly and **managers are increasingly reluctant to put their neck on the line for a risky project, purchase or vendor**. This is having a major impact on the nature of decision-making. Indeed, the buying process, with its emphasis on planning, consultation and analysis, is in effect a risk management process.

Buyers tell us that they are most sensitive to risk when the following factors are present:

- The buying decision is new (as opposed to, for example, a repeat purchase).
- The buying decision has major consequences, is high profile or big budget.
- The vendor is not well known or another vendor owns the account.
- The product, process or technology involved is new.
- The buying decision is politically sensitive.
- The buying group is large.

So, salespeople need to be aware where any of these factors are present. However, they also need to be aware that risk comes in many forms. That is because **the risk of choosing the wrong supplier is often not the greatest risk** when it comes to major buying decisions.

Regardless of the choice of provider and solution, there are many other factors (business, technology and project-related risks, for example) that may impinge on the achievement of the required outcome. So, **the salesperson cannot be solely concerned with convincing the buyer their solution will deliver on its promises**, but must also demonstrate how the solution will enable the buyer to achieve the outcomes they expect.

The business case must include scenarios and probabilities as regards results and outcomes. It must also include a register of risk, listing each risk, rating it and outlining how it is to be managed. So, if a salesperson's proposal is going to mirror the business case of the buyer it has to add risk into the equation. The issue of risk is discussed in more detail in **Part 2, Section 10: The Sales Orders Revolution**.

Compliance Issues

The business case must also address risk-related elements, such as details of implementation, governance and control. In particular it must address issues of compliance — whether that is adherence to internal standards or external regulation. This clearly is a factor that is growing in importance.

Strategic Fit

So, when the numbers stack up and an attractive payback is evident, even making allowance for risk and compliance, is the result a compelling business case? Perhaps not, because managers must demonstrate that the project fits with the pre-existing jig-saw of organizational priorities, goals and strategies. They must demonstrate the purchase will help the organization to achieve its objectives and boost its performance.

In short, with a diverse portfolio of projects and purchases competing for scarce organizational resources, managers must be able to demonstrate that their purchase or project is more relevant and compelling than others.

Taking all these factors into consideration it is possible to **create a consistent universal formula for the business case**. While the language and terminology used may vary from company to company, a business case will be based on the following formula:

This represents only the skeleton, as a lot more back-up and supporting information is likely to be added. That may include a summary of market information, supplier quotes, technical analysis and so on.

The Essential Building Blocks

The term business case can mean different things to different people. For this reason it is helpful to explain the key elements of a business case in terms of other more universally understood business planning and analysis tools. The business case combines four elements as shown in the diagram.

The B2B Revolution   Section 3

Fig. 3.3: The Building Blocks of the Business Case

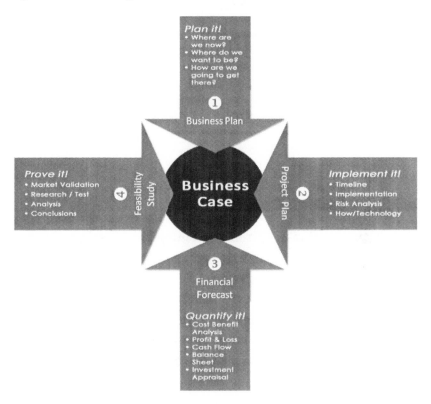

Considering the business case along the four dimensions above provides a broader perspective. For example, many business cases are good at explaining what they want to do (1), but fall short in terms of proof/validation (2), or financial quantification (3), or how the project will be delivered (4). Because the seller is concerned with the business case the sales proposal must also contain these four elements.

The business case must address the needs of multiple audiences, ranging from the CEO to the COO. This again is reflective of the scope of what is involved. Of course the business case may also reference other elements such as a technical audit or supplier analysis, however, these are the items that tend not to be overlooked by sellers.

Would you be surprised to know that many large organizations require a business case for purchases of as little as €20,000?   As one UK veteran salesperson told us recently, 'I have seen more business cases in the past year than I have in the previous 19 years.' There is more strategic business logic being applied to buying decisions than ever before.

Building A Business Case

It would be a mistake to see the business case as just another administrative document needed to get approval. Sophisticated buying groups see the process for creating the business case as being as important as the business case itself. In these organizations the business case is really **a framework for planning, decision-making, implementation and review**. It has a full project lifespan, increasingly starting well in advance of the purchase and ending only after project success is achieved.

The business case is a living and breathing entity that grows in sophistication over time, from the preliminary document created at the outset and easily summarized on one or two pages to a comprehensive document with financials in tow.

A business case is an economic argument for investing in a project or purchase. However, **it is not purely economic, but also political.** In this context the successful business case will involve a process of extensive involvement with stakeholders and will be written, or at least reviewed, by cross-functional committees. This is essential to creating the buy-in that is likely to be required to get the project sanctioned as well as to ensure it can be successfully implemented.

Once the purchase decision is made, best practice dictates the business case is used to track implementation and project success. It is also updated as required to reflect the changing conditions in the organization and its environment.

'Playing it safe' is built into the design of the buying process by means of the steps, consultation, multiple decision-makers, documentation and signoffs around the business case.

A robust business case must also examine a number of alternatives, in order to arrive at the best or recommended solution. After all, if this does not take place, the business case has already in some ways predetermined the outcome.

SELLER INSIGHT

'Are vendors focused on writing sales proposals really helping buyers to buy? After all, it is the business case that matters. Buyers must take pen to paper and justify their planned purchase in a document that will be scrutinized dispassionately by many others in their organization. It must calculate the costs, benefits and risk equation of their project — often to a level of sophistication that would impress a university professor. The buying decision will live or die based on its business case.'

Senior Salesperson

The Role Of The Business Case

So, why is the business case so important? Well, the key reasons the business case is now at the center of major buying decisions are listed below. The business case:

- <u>Drives business success</u>: It ensures any projects, purchases or investments enable the organization to achieve its objectives.
- <u>Allocates scarce resources</u> to maximum effect to get the best economic return. Projects must compete for funding.
- <u>Ensures better and more careful decisions</u>, for example:
  - More structure, rigor and discipline around decisions.
  - Focuses on results, including ROI/Payback.
  - Takes the 'personality' out of the purchase decision.
  - Minimizes the extent of politics involved.
  - Ensures decisions are consistent with business strategy and goals.
  - Manages exposure to risk.
- <u>Prevents canvassing</u>: It manages the process of interaction with suppliers, preventing undue influence and in some cases keeps suppliers at arms length. It also ensures the fairness of the buying process.
- <u>Ensures compliance</u> with internal and external standards, regulations and directives.
- <u>Builds consensus</u>: In a way the process of building the business case is a means of ensuring key stakeholders are involved and consulted. All major projects involve change, and the business case process is an important first step in change management.
- <u>Maximizes project success</u> in the following ways:
  - Ensures projects are more thoroughly planned.
  - Ensures a <u>common understanding</u> of projects and decisions.
  - Provides a framework against which project success can be <u>measured and reviewed</u>.
  - Ensures managers and suppliers are <u>accountable</u>.

Thus, the salesperson who helps to shape and influence the business case has a real opportunity to help the buyer and thereby to stand apart from competitors.

The Business Case And The Crystal Ball

Predicting the future is not easy, but that is exactly what the business case must attempt to do. This is particularly true in a time of market turbulence. Today's perfect plan could be completely invalidated by a change in the competitive situation, an upset in the market or any one of a host of other factors outside the company's control.

However, when it boils down to it, there are three reasons why business cases get it wrong and the manager's best-laid plans are foiled. You can think of them as *Three Temptations*. That is the temptation to:

1. Underestimate costs.

2. Exaggerate benefits.

3. Underestimate the time required.

Most business cases fall victim to at least one of these problems. For example, in the area of IT projects it is regularly documented that 80% of projects fail. For this reason any business case should be subjected to sensitivity analysis in respect of these three key variables (as well as others). Thus a key question for the salesperson to help the buyer address is: **'What would be the impact of a 5%, 10% or 15% variance in terms of the benefits, costs, or timing?'**

When Temptations Are Greatest

Even with the greatest of management science, predicting the future can be a challenge. However, it is when there is more subjectivity than science that the temptations are at their strongest. This can happen in particular where:

- There is a powerful project sponsor (manager or department).
- Politics or vested interests are involved.
- There is urgency — most businesses don't make their best decisions in a crisis.
- There is an element of vanity associated with the project.
- Stakeholders are attempting to justify past decisions.
- There is a high degree of risk and uncertainty involved.
- The decision is a new one (with no precedent or past experience).
- Clarity of plans, strategies and goals does not exist.
- The buying process is weak.

The salesperson must look out for all of the above factors as they make the success of even a compelling business case uncertain. When these factors are evident it is vitally important the salesperson follows steps to ensure that more accurate and objective business case financials can be prepared.

How To Ensure More Accurate Estimates

Business case decisions are not always going to be right, after all predicting the future is an imperfect science. All forecasts are simply estimates, which are in essence a sophisticated form of guesswork. However, the business case can increase accuracy by following these steps:

- State assumptions clearly.
- Test and validate assumptions.
- Examine alternatives.
- Present a number of scenarios.
- Include feasibility study type market/other data.
- Incorporate benchmarking data.
- Perform a sensitivity analysis.
- Allow for a contingency.
- Present an analysis and quantification of risks.
- Have the business case reviewed by experts.

The seller must leverage each of the above steps in terms of their influence over the buyer's business case. This is particularly important given the skepticism among buyers of vendor ROI models (something that is discussed in Section 9 of The Selling Revolution™).

Applying Business Case Principles

With the overview of the logic of the business decision now complete, we now recommend you take a few minutes to apply what has been discussed to your key sales opportunities. To do this a checklist is presented overleaf. It will guide you to aspects of the business case that may require attention and by so doing help you to maximize your chances of winning the deal.

In the next section (**Section 4: The Buying Team Revolution**) we will examine the revolution in terms of who makes the buying decision. In particular we will see, because decisions are made higher and wider, the importance of the business case has rapidly increased.

How well do you know the business case involved in your major sales opportunities?

BUSINESS CASE: __WHY__ the decision is going to be made:

CHECKLIST

	I am Sure	I am Not Sure

1. Is a business case required? If yes:
  • What format will it take?
  • Who is responsible for drafting it?
  • Is there a template to be followed?
	☐	☐

2. What is the buying organisation trying to achieve?	☐	☐
3. What are the key business drivers and metrics?	☐	☐
4. What ROI / Payback will be required?	☐	☐
5. What are the broader strategic issues at play?	☐	☐
6. Are there competing projects / alternatives?	☐	☐
7. What level of risk is associated with the decision?	☐	☐
8. What past decisions bear on the decision?	☐	☐
9. What governance or compliance issues are relevant?	☐	☐

ACTIONS

Rate out of 10 Your Knowledge of Business Case

_____

How well do you feel your sales approach and proposition address the business case (Out of 10)

_____

BUSINESS CASE
WHY?
REVOLUTION

The Business Case Revolution — Summary

Major purchase decisions are first and foremost important business decisions. They are generally part of a larger project or bigger strategy. In essence, they are just one piece of the larger organizational jigsaw.

That means major buying decisions must be underpinned by indisputable business logic, communicated in the international language of numbers. Planning and analysis have supplanted impulse, discretion and emotion. This has been driven by the requirements of the business case.

Buyers must calculate the costs, benefits and risks equation of their project often to a level of sophistication that would impress a university professor. Their proposal will then live or die based on its business case.

There are many implications for the seller, including:

- Vendors must ask how they can impact on the performance and further the strategic goals of the buyer's business. They must see the bigger picture — that is the sale in its wider project or strategy context.
- Vendors must understand all of the buyer's options and alternatives, including competing projects, the option of doing it in-house or even delaying a decision.
- Instead of writing sales proposals, vendors must help buyers to build the business case.

SECTION 4:

The Buying Team Revolution

WHO MAKES TODAY'S BUYING DECISIONS

It is not enough that The Buying Revolution™ has transformed how, as well as why buying decisions are made. The demographics and psychographics of the modern buyer have fundamentally changed too.

The result is that sellers looking in the usual places to find today's new buyers are being disappointed. Those who have successfully found these new buyers, but expect them to respond like the old ones will come to rue their error of judgment.

This section examines the new profile and attitudes of the extended buying team, including the implications for how we as salespeople sell.

The New Atlas Of Buying

At one time a question, such as 'who makes the buying decision?' was easy to answer. Typically, one or two names were sufficient to describe where the power lay. But this is no longer the case. Sellers almost need a map of organizational buying to reflect all those who make and shape the buying decision.

The result is sellers can easily end up talking to the wrong people or even to the right people about the wrong things. This is particularly the case where sellers are focused solely on selling to those individuals who freely made buying decisions in the past.

Managers Are Straight-Jacketed

Sellers are slowly realizing the age of the buyer as a free agent is over. Individual managers can no longer simply write a check or sign a purchase order. They have been straight-jacketed by purchase procedures and their autonomy regarding purchase decisions greatly diminished. Buyers tell us that:

- Managers have had their <u>sign-off thresholds lowered</u> and, in many cases, as much as halved.
- Even small <u>purchases must be signed-off</u> and it is no longer a matter of senior managers 'rubber-stamping' requests.
- All purchase decisions are <u>being increasingly scrutinized</u> at a local, regional and even global level before approval is granted.
- There is a mounting <u>burden of proof</u> on managers who want to get sign-off on major purchases, as well much smaller ones. Managers must:
  - o Demonstrate their plans are in keeping with <u>changed organizational priorities</u> and strategies.
  - o <u>Show immediate and tangible results</u> — that is the quantifiable impact on key business performance metrics.

- Jump through hoops to get projects and purchases approved. That means more paperwork, committees and sign-offs are required for purchases managers previously had authority to approve. Indeed, purchases for as little as 10 or 20k may require the presentation of a mini business case. The locus of control in respect of buying has shifted from the individual to the organization.

Redrawing The Map Of Organizational Buying

Buying power has shifted in large organizations. It has moved down the hall, spread out across the organization and moved up in the elevator to the most senior levels. As shown in the diagram overleaf decisions are being made higher and wider in most organizations.

The center of control for buying decisions in most organizations has changed considerably. In a seemingly contradictory fashion, organizational buying decisions have become more democratic and autocratic at once.

While the buying process requires greater cross-functional teamwork and consultation with stakeholders, the ultimate power to make decisions has ascended to the top ranks of most large organizations.

Fig. 4.1: Where are today's buyers to be found?

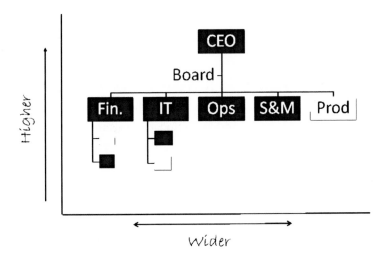

The excerpt below highlights the number of levels involved in the buying decision, the seniority of the decision makers as well as the importance of functional buying teams.

Fig. 4.2: Decision levels in the *Fortune 1000* buying process

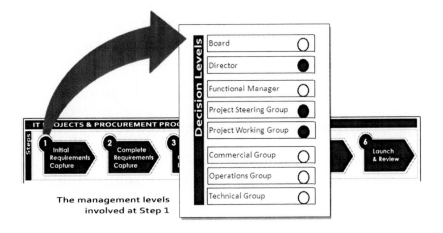

This is a clear example of buying taking place higher and wider across a *Fortune 1000* organization. This buying process involves anywhere up to 50 people in various groups and committees depending on the value of the purchase and there are often as many as five parties to the buying decision:

1. A **working group** driving the purchase decision and responsible for completing the various steps (e.g. the business plan, the requirements document and outlining the business case), backed up by a more **heavy-weight steering group** whose purpose is to oversee the process and keep it on track. These teams are cross-functional in make up.

2. Those involved in reviewing the project at key stages — in this example there are **commercial, technical and operations groups** — whose role is to ensure congruence with existing plans, strategies and objectives in each of the areas in question.

3. A range of **stakeholders** consulted during the process across all departments, from users to end-customers. This process of consultation is essential in ensuring organization-wide buy-in and support. Examples include consultation in terms of the development of the use case, customer case and business case (Step 1) and with channel partners as well as sales and marketing (Step 3). These can be seen by reference to the complete buying process map shown in Section 2.

4. The ultimate **power brokers**, often at director and board level, who act as the final arbitrators of the business case. They are responsible for the final sign-off or official sanction of the purchase.

5. The **stewards of the buying process** are to be found in the purchasing department. Their new role is to develop professional purchasing processes and skills throughout the organization to support business buyers, protecting them from wayward sellers.

The involvement of the different parties varies according to the stage of the buying process as shown in the diagram below.

Fig. 4.3: Who is Involved At Each Stage of the Buying Process

IT PROJECTS & PROCUREMENT PROCESS (major projects)					
1 Initial Requirements Capture	**2** Complete Requirements Capture	**3** Business Case & High Level Design	**4** Detailed Design	**5** Build & Test	**6** Launch & Review
Board ○		●			●
Director ●	○	●	○	●	●
Functional Manager ○	●	●	●	●	●
Project Steering Group ●	●	●	●	●	●
Project Working Group ●	●	●	●	●	●
Commercial Group ○	○	●	○	●	●
Operations Group ○	○	●	○	●	●
Technical Group ○	○	●	●	●	○

Regarding who is involved and when, there are some interesting points to note:

- The project working group, backed up by the project steering group, is at the center of the process through all the steps.
- Most levels are involved in at least an oversight role throughout the process (denoted by the outline circle).
- The most extensive involvement across all parties is at the Business Case and High-level Design (stage 3) phase as well as during Launch and Review (stage 6).
- The board is involved at the critical go-ahead junction at the end of phase 3 — that is the Business Case. It is also involved in reviewing conformance with the business case at the close of stage 6: Launch and Review.

So, what are the implications of decisions taking place at higher and wider levels in the organization? Well there are many, but let us examine some of the key ones now.

When Buyers Pull Rank

When it comes to major buying decisions, managers are pulling rank. Senior managers are not just rubber-stamping buying decisions. They are taking an active role to ensure all major purchases underpin organizational goals, priorities and strategies. All this means the job titles of those involved in making today's major buying decisions are impressive. So too are their CVs. These increasingly grey-haired managers are more qualified and more experienced than ever before. To compound the problem, they are busier and carry greater levels of responsibility.

The implication is that salespeople must climb higher in the organization in order to get the sale. However, that can present challenges as starting a conversation with C-Level management is not easy. Getting past the PA is only one aspect of the challenge. For example, at this higher altitude the air is thinner and the salesperson's features and benefits message may struggle to survive. A new level of confidence and skill is required to be able to relate to the senior manager.

Naturally enough senior managers make different purchases than their lower-level colleagues. From their offices on the top floor they can see the 'bigger picture'. They have a clearer understanding of key business drivers, priorities and strategies that comes from being closer to the boardroom. Rather than reading the technical manual or detailed specification, they want to talk results and discuss strategy. As others have put it, the challenge in selling at this level requires more than just a salesperson, but rather a 'business person who sells'.

Buying As A Team Sport

The modern buyer is a team, not an individual. Indeed, as the example shown earlier suggests, the roll call of all those involved in the buying decision is a veritable 'who's who' of the organization.

As we can see in the example, although the purchase involved IT, the technical buyer is only one of many voices at the buying table. Indeed, if the purchase is big enough, it will go to the board for approval.

Modern buying requires more committees and consensus. Indeed, those buyers and sellers we talked to suggest that the numbers involved in major buying decisions has doubled in a decade. Multifunctional buying teams are the order of the day, together with a high level of consultation and involvement for all stakeholders.

Of course more people involved in the process means more politics and requires reconciling a greater diversity of personalities and viewpoints. This is something that elongates buying cycles and from the seller's point of view increases the degree of uncertainty involved.

So, the buying decision is not a solo run, it is a team effort. The only problem is that the seller is rarely a part of the buyer's team. Indeed, they may have little or no contact with the majority of those making or shaping the decision. In this context, selling, just like buying, is no longer a one-man job. It requires a pairing of executives from both buyer and seller in an effective team-based approach to selling.

New Buyer Attitudes

As the locus of buying control has changed, the very character of buying has been transformed. Much of the frustration felt by the traditional salesperson results because today's buyers are more sophisticated, skeptical and self-contained than ever before. Indeed, there is a new manifesto among today's buyers:

Fig. 4.4: The Manifesto for the New Buyer

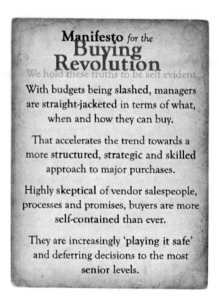

Let's examine the attitudes of today's new buyers:

(a) Buyers Are More Sophisticated

The day when the salesperson knew more than the buyer is over. Indeed, the situation is often reversed. That is especially true given the increasingly grey-haired nature of those making today's buying decisions.

Buyers often know more than the seller, although they can be coy about showing it. They may know the answers, but that does not stop them asking the questions and as a result putting the seller to the test.

In addition, buyers are no longer dependent on the salesperson as a source of information. Buyers now have greater access to a wide variety of sources, including analysts, buying forums and the web. This often means the buyer may know more than the salesperson about the products or solutions available.

As a result buyers are more confident about what they want, as well as what they don't. They no longer go 'cap in hand' to vendors looking for a solution, nor do they accept vendor information on face value.

(b) Buyers Are More Skeptical

Those involved in today's buying decisions have seen it all before — the presentations and promises, as well as the all too frequent disappointments. These past experiences have given rise to a certain weariness of sellers.

For every good salesperson buyers have dealt with there have been several bad ones. Unfortunately, it is the bad ones that have shaped buyer opinions of the profession. The sins of past salespeople are carried forward and those in the profession today must make amends.

BUYER INSIGHT

B

What Buyers Think Of Salespeople

We asked hundreds of managers to describe the typical salesperson. Here are their most frequent words used:

Talks too much	Unprepared
Doesn't listen	Lacks product/industry knowledge
Pushy	Unpunctual
False/Insincere	Interrupts
Know-all/Show-off	Not trustworthy
Rude/Bad Manners	

The reality is that buyers have learned not to trust 'the typical salesperson'. This also applies to seller propaganda, in the form of value statements, sales pitches and marketing brochures. For example, buyers regularly complain that:

- <u>Salespeople are too careless with their promises</u> — making more of them than they can keep. For example, when the buyer asks, 'Can your solution do X?' or 'Does it do Y?' and 'What about Z?' the answer is a surprising 'YES' to everything. Not surprisingly the buyer is wary.
- <u>Sellers are making the same universal claims</u> — that leads buyers to respond 'everybody says that'. Just visit the websites of any three vendors in the same industry to see how confusingly similar seller claims can be.
- <u>The speed at which a seller arrives at a solution</u> often results in question marks about the level of understanding of or empathy for the buyer's needs.
- Salespeople continue to use <u>crude and manipulative sales techniques</u> from the 'standing room only' close to the 'good cop, bad cop' negotiating ploy.

The result is that taking the salesperson's 'word for it' is something buyers are reluctant to do. They are less interested in what the salesperson claims and more interested in what customers who have used the solution have to say. They want case studies and credible whitepapers, as opposed to marketing speak and glossy brochures.

BUYER INSIGHT

B

Six Ways Buyers Can Defeat A Seller's Ploys

The game is on between the cautious buyer and wily seller. Here are some of the tips employed by buyers as a result:

1. **Silence is golden.** Be guarded in terms of sharing information with vendors regarding budget, timeline, criticality and your organizational chart.

2. **Don't be so grateful.** Don't fall for the special treatment and don't feel indebted to the vendor for any trip, seminar or event.

3. **Don't drink and buy.** No matter how much you think you can handle your alcohol, never drink with a vendor.

4. **Maintain your own pace.** Don't be encouraged to speed up or slow down your process by the vendor.

5. **Set The Rules of Engagement.** Set out what contact with salespeople is appropriate at the different stages of the buying process.

6. **Thanks, but no thanks.** Ensure clear written policies with respect to vendor gifts.

(c) Buyers Are More Self-Contained

The new buyer is more independent and this means seller marketing is struggling to make an impact. It is only the very special salesperson that will get through. That is because buyers have learned to <u>use the tools of the unwitting salesperson in their own defense</u>. For example:

- Keeping a salesperson at bay by requesting further information, documentation or even a proposal.
- Stalling an over-enthusiastic tele-salesperson by requesting a brochure in the post.

The various attitudinal changes on the part of buyers (as listed above) mean the seller must move beyond traditional features and benefits selling. They must demonstrate the ability to input in a meaningful way to the buyer's product requirements and, more importantly, to the business case. Doing this effectively requires a metamorphosis on the part of the salesperson. As we will see in Part 2 – The Sales Revolution™, it means 'bye-bye salesperson, hello trusted advisor'.

Applying The Buying Team Principles

With our overview of how the buying team has changed complete, we recommend that you take a few minutes to apply the issues addressed to your key pipeline opportunities. To guide you we have provided a template overleaf to highlight aspects of the buying team that may require attention.

How well do you know the buying process involved in your major sales opportunities? To find out apply the following questions to your sales opportunities.

BUYING PROCESS: <u>HOW</u> the decision is going to be made:

BUYING A PROCESS REVOLUTION

CHECKLIST	I am Sure	I am Not Sure	ACTIONS
1. What is the buying process?	☐	☐	
2. How rigid, structured, or sophisticated is it?	☐	☐	
3. What are the key steps?	☐	☐	
4. What are the key review/sign-off points?	☐	☐	
5. How long will it take?	☐	☐	
6. What stage in the buying process is the purchase at?	☐	☐	
• Have requirements been defined?			
• Has a business case been created?			
• Has a budget been allocated?			
• Is there a shortlist of vendors? How many? What criterion?			
7. What documentation is required by the buying unit?	☐	☐	

Rate out of 10 Your Buying Process Knowledge _____

☐

How well do you feel the buying process has been facilitated by your sales approach: (Out of 10) _____

The Buying Team Revolution — Summary

BUYING TEAM REVOLUTION

Buying decisions are being made higher and wider in most large organizations, with consequences such as longer and more unpredictable sales cycles. The salesperson must now interact with cross-functional buying teams and increasingly 'grey-haired' managers.

Sellers must deal with buyers that know as much, if not more than the salesperson and are cautious, if not wary, of their dealings with sellers. Engaging with these new buyers requires a metamorphosis on the part of the salesperson.

SECTION 5:

The Ideological Revolution

EXPLODING THE MYTHS OF BUYING & SELLING

When New Buying Meets Old Selling

We have seen how buying decisions are made, now it is time to explode some myths about selling that make old selling and new buying so difficult to reconcile.

Myth #1: It's about selling.

Myth #2: The seller is in control.

Myth #3: The unsophisticated buyer.

Myth #4: Buyers want to be sold to.

Myth #5: It is a buying decision.

Myth #6: Buyers want products or services.

Myth #7: It's about selecting a supplier.

Myth #8: Sales process equals buying process.

Myth #9: The competition is another supplier.

Myth #10: The purchase order is everything.

Myth #11: The purchasing department pushes paper.

These myths form part of the popular folklore of selling. They are the equivalent of flying saucers, Bermuda Triangles and Loch Ness Monsters of selling. Yet, they often go unquestioned and as salespeople we all cling to at least three or four of these beliefs. The problem is that **just as thought precedes action, these beliefs determine our sales strategies and behaviors**. So, to change we must tackle these myths.

Buying Myths

To quote Einstein, 'The significant problems we face cannot be solved by the same level of thinking we were at when we created them.' In other words, the problem of getting buyers to buy cannot be solved with out-of-date thinking about selling.

What sellers can achieve through new sales productivity, sales process and sales skills initiatives is limited, unless the maps, paradigms and beliefs underpinning much of traditional selling are revised to reflect the new realities of modern buying.

On the other hand, sellers who stubbornly hold on to these beliefs are doomed to a spiral of diminishing sales effectiveness and falling conversion rates. The writing is on the wall — **The Buying Revolution™ has turned the traditional views of selling on their head**. Over the following pages we will deconstruct each of these myths one at a time.

1. It's About Selling

Many sellers have spent too long on one side of the table to be able to relate to buyers and exactly what they are thinking. They need to stop looking at selling through a sales-centered lens.

(a) It's About Buying!

'It's the economy, stupid!' is a phrase that played an important role in the election of Bill Clinton as US President in 1992. Proof that stating the obvious is very important.

Now, we have been in selling for decades, we have read thousands of sales books, we have talked with hundreds of salespeople, attended some of the most costly sales training workshops and guess what, nobody has ever stated the obvious — It's about buying! They have talked little about how organizations buy, such as how buying decisions are made or who makes them. We have sat through hundreds of opportunity and pipeline reviews where knowledge of the stage of the buying decision, the buying unit or the buying criteria was sorely lacking. The only conclusion we can arrive at is that **the sales profession has been too busy selling to think much about buying**. An exaggerated view of the prowess of the salesperson is a part of the problem.

(b) The Salesperson-Centric View Of Selling

You have heard it all before — a good salesperson can sell sand to the Arabs, ice to the Eskimos and even Christmas to Turkeys. Indeed, you have heard it so often that at least some part of you believes it to be true.

But if a good salesperson is what matters most and if such a good salesperson can sell anything regardless of buyers and their requirements, then that means that everything we have talked about regarding modern buying is irrelevant. The only problem is that **the natural magic of the salesperson is not enough** to:

- Navigate today's complex buying processes.
- Shape the business case upon which the purchase decision will be made.
- Gain access to the executive suite or boardroom where the decision is going to be made.

Indeed, most of what was considered the black art of selling is lost on buyers, who generally take a pretty dim view of salespeople. Indeed, as we will see later, one of the key challenges for the salesperson is to distance themselves from the stereotypical seller in the eyes of the buyer. To help the buyer to buy the salesperson needs to be something more.

(c) Helping The Buyer To Buy

The solution to getting buyers to buy is not selling. **Buyers may want to buy, but that does not mean that they want to be sold to**. Indeed, that is often the last thing that they want. They don't want to be treated as a lead or prospect, and they don't want to be prequalified or closed. Nor do they want to be corralled into the salesperson's sales pipeline or funnel. The seller's role has changed — it is to help the buyer to buy.

2: THE SELLER IS IN CONTROL

Perhaps the greatest myth of all in respect of selling
relates to who is in control. It is widely believed that
the seller can or should be in control. However,
nothing is further from the truth.

The Seller As The Center Of The Universe

Notice anything wrong with the diagram below? Well, as out of place
with reality as it may seem it describes pretty well the traditional view
of selling.

Fig. 5.1: The Mistaken View - Seller At the Center

We call it Ptolemy's Theory of Selling — inspired by Ptolemy's belief
that the Earth was at the center of the universe and that everything
else revolved around it.

However, **the seller is not the center of the universe**, so no amount of
sales process, marketing hype or vanity on the part of the salesperson
can change that. Selling requires a new world view, one that puts the
buyer at the centre.

Fig. 5.2: The Corrected View – Buyer at the Centre

When the new science of buying meets the traditional art of selling there are going to be problems. Organizational buying once ad hoc and unstructured has become highly sophisticated and process-driven. The result is that sales process must take second place to the rigid and demanding processes buyers must follow if purchase decisions are to be sanctioned.

Sellers are not in control, nor should they be. It is time salespeople gave up on the false idea of controlling the buyer. After all, if the buyer is not in control then the project is unlikely to get approval. Indeed, if the buyer is not in control then they are by default not senior or experienced enough to be taken seriously.

For the seller **control is a dangerous illusion**. This illusion is all too evident in their off-the-shelf sales proposals and clumsy closing techniques that alienate buyers, as well as a variety of dangerous assumptions that lead to surprises, sales cycle setbacks and unreliable sales forecasts.

Buyers Have Seized Control

The term 'Caveat Emptor', or buyer beware, was the dominant concept for decades. But the balance of power has shifted, with the seller reluctantly ceding control to a more sophisticated and cynical breed of buyer. Today it is the seller who must beware.

Increasingly, the buyer's philosophy is **'if you don't manage the vendor, the vendor will manage you**'. As a consequence the salesperson is increasingly left on the outside looking in.

Buyers know they have the power in a market where suppliers out-number customers. They are increasingly confident and assertive in dealing with vendors. In short, they call all the shots. They like to be in control and stay in control. That means they start to elicit the requirements, build the business case and define the solution well in advance of meeting vendors.

The seller is no longer 'the ringmaster' of the sale, often being reduced to the role of a mere spectator. This is particularly the case where buyers are turning to the competitive tendering process (i.e. RFPs, RFIs and RFQs) to keep suppliers at arms length during the selection process.

New Rules Of Engagement

When it comes to buying there are new rules at play, fixed and immutable rules, such as the requirements of the buying process or the business case. The seller cannot break these rules, but these rules can break the seller.

Buyers now define what contact between buyer and seller is appropriate, even permissible, at each stage of the buying process. They are controlling access to managers with responses such as: 'You will have to go through purchasing' or 'If you tell me the information that you need I will get it for you.' **They don't take well to vendors who try to circumvent the rules or go over their head. The fact is many** sellers are left waiting in the hallway, while decisions are being made behind closed doors.

Buyers are also controlling access to information with the implication being that sellers are often required to prepare proposals based on mere guesswork or assumption.

#3: THE UNSOPHISTICATED BUYER

It can be tempting to underestimate the buyer — to assume they know less or are less sophisticated than the seller. Increasingly, this is a dangerous assumption. As we discussed in the previous section today's buyers often know more than the sales team selling to them. They are exercising greater care in how decisions are made.

One seller explained the challenge in this way: 'Our customers have got better at buying, something that has taken many of us sellers by surprise. Perhaps this is a reality that many of us would rather not come to terms with. It challenges the status-quo and threatens the very survival of many sellers.'

Appreciating and even embracing the complexity of modern buying is key to sales success in today's markets. As salespeople we need to come to grips with the changed nature of organizational buying and transform our sales approach accordingly. We have to ensure we don't underestimate the buyer and start re-engineering our self-serving sales processes to sync with how decisions are now made.

You may ask yourself is there a danger of ascribing too much intelligence and sophistication to the buyer? In our experience **it is better to over, as opposed to under-estimate the level of sophistication of the buyer** or the level of complexity of the buying decision. To do so ensures that as a professional salesperson you are always prepared.

So, if the buying processes described in this book appear to be more sophisticated than those in evidence in the organizations to which you sell today, very likely their existing processes will, in the near future become more sophisticated. If the buyer is not asking the salesperson for a ROI analysis, that does not mean that its power to close the sale is in any way diminished. After all the objective of the salesperson is to help the buyer to buy, that includes helping less sophisticated buyers also. Unless the salesperson helps the buyer to adopt best-practice principles of buying, the likelihood of getting the purchase sanctioned will be diminished.

4: Buyers Want To Be Sold To

A typical mistake made by salespeople is to assume that buyers want to be sold to. **Buyers may want to buy, but that does not mean they want to be sold to**.

Indeed, as noted earlier, that is often the last thing that they want. They don't want to be treated as a lead, a suspect or a prospect, and they don't want to be prequalified or closed. Nor do they want to be corralled into the salesperson's sales pipeline or funnel.

Revenue-starved vendors have become increasingly aggressive in the search of new customers. Buyers are facing more of what they have learned to distrust and even dread — cold calls, sales pitches, invitations to events and so on. They have responded by retreating behind voicemail, spam filters, no-names policies and competitive tendering processes.

They are keeping salespeople at bay by requesting further information, documentation or even a proposal. They are stalling over-enthusiastic telesalespeople by requesting brochures in the post.

5: IT IS A BUYING DECISION

It is all about the buying decision, right? Well it used to be, but not anymore. **Today's major purchase requires not just a buying decision** but a more fundamental business decision.

Saying that a major purchase is a business, as opposed to a buying decision is not just a play on words. The two are dramatically different. The six stage buying process examined earlier demonstrates this clearly — the process has all the hallmarks of a complex business decision. Take for example the level of planning involved. It is what one might associate with the decision to enter a new market or launch a new product.

The business decision is complex, as well as strategic. It is concerned with business goals, strategies and results. Buying decisions on the other hand tend to be more narrowly focused in terms of suppliers and specifications. The former therefore clearly requires a different type of selling to the latter.

Major purchasing decisions made by managers and their departments can have important strategic implications for the entire organization. So it is no surprise that business decision-making and project-planning principles are being applied or that managers are required to demonstrate how their purchases will drive business performance.

The buying process in respect of major purchases is in fact **a 'full-on' business decision-making and planning process**.

6: BUYERS BUY PRODUCTS & SERVICES

Most salespeople are still selling products and services. That is in spite of the fact that what buyers really want are solutions to problems, not products and services.

Take a look back at the buying process examined in Section 3. How many times does it talk about product or service? Certainly a lot less than it talks about the business case and requirements.

Buyers want to achieve results, to exploit opportunities and address challenges facing their business. Their primary interest is not a product or service and its features and benefits, but rather the results that can be achieved. Again this is clearly demonstrated in the buying model example. Although it relates to the purchase of IT, **it is clearly not just a technology decision**. Rather **it is a business decision** regarding technology.

So, while the vendor involved in this process may be selling technology, the buyer is planning the future success of their business. That means the decision:

- Won't be made based on the basis of the technology's features (something vendors often forget) but on its business advantages.
- Will revolve around numbers in the business case, not feature lists in a technical specification document.
- Will not rest in the hands of the IT or Operations Department. The buying decision will be made by a cross-functional group of senior managers and will involve extensive consultation with all the stakeholders involved, from users to end-customers.

7: IT'S ABOUT SELECTING A SUPPLIER

Salespeople expect the *Fortune 1000* buying process to focus on 'shopping for a supplier' and to include such steps as:

- Defining vendor selection criteria.
- Short-listing vendors.
- Briefing shortlisted vendors.
- Eliciting vendor proposals.
- Vendor presentations and clarifications.
- Vendor selection.
- Notification of successful and unsuccessful vendors.
- Final negotiation of terms and signing of contract.

But these steps are not listed. Although an inevitable part of any procurement process, they are too obvious. Perhaps it is because they are subsidiary to the other steps, such as the definition of requirements or the business case.

Buyers are quick to remind us that **selecting a supplier is after all only a small part of the buying process**, perhaps even the smallest part. Think of it this way, the reason projects don't go ahead is not because the buyer cannot select between competing vendors, but most likely because a compelling business case has not been established and approved.

#8: Sales Process Equals Buying Process

It follows that as selecting a supplier is only a small part of the process, the sales process is typically only a small part of the buying process.

The buying process is not just the search for a supplier and it does not begin by talking to suppliers about their solutions. It often begins long before the seller becomes involved and may even continue after the seller has departed.

As shown below it is not until the third phase of the *Fortune 1000* buying process that suppliers are explicitly mentioned and then only to 'obtain supplier quotes'.

Fig. 5.3: Buying Process: The Seller Is in the Dark

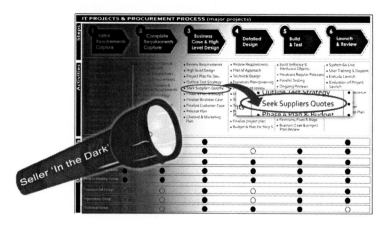

For more than one-third of the buying process (the most important part) the seller is in the dark and has yet to be called to the table. **Effectively the role of the seller has been marginalized.** As this example shows the seller is no longer required until requirements have been defined and the business case is well underway.

As a result of not being involved until relatively late in the buying process it becomes more difficult for suppliers to differentiate themselves or to even influence the buyer's decision criteria. Indeed, they risk being drawn into a competitive bidding situation.

Clearly, **the buying process is no longer defined by the interaction with the seller**. Indeed, the sales process and the buying process are two very distinct things, as shown in the next diagram.

Fig. 5.4: Overlaying Sales Process on The Buying Process

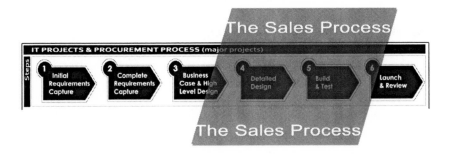

When the vendor's sales process is overlaid on the buyer's buying process it highlights a stark difference in perspective. The buyer's view is long-term and strategic, whereas the seller's is short-term and often focused purely on completing the sale.

9: THE COMPETITION IS
ANOTHER SUPPLIER

Sellers mistakenly assume that the competition is
another supplier. However, in most cases it is not.
The real competition is another project vying for the same resources, a
decision to delay, a decision not to proceed or to do it in-house.

With pressure on budgets, projects and purchases must compete for
scarce organizational resources. Manager-buyers must demonstrate
that their project merits support over competing projects based on a
compelling business case and demonstrable strategic fit.

The seller's narrow view of 'the competition' can be dangerous. It
results in focusing on the competitive advantages of the seller's
solution, as well as its capability and track record. These are factors
that have only marginal impact on the buying decision. After all there
is no point being in pole position for a deal that will never go ahead.
Indeed, the number one reason why deals don't proceed is not
because of the challenge of picking the right supplier, but because a
compelling business case has not been established.

Real differentiation between suppliers is not simply about competitive
advantages, but the ability to help the buyer to build a compelling
business case.

#10: THE PO IS EVERYTHING

For most salespeople the purchase order is both the alpha and the omega, the beginning and the end. The problem is that buyers see things very differently.

Where Is The Purchase Order?

By searching through the detail of the activities set out in Section 2, we see that the PO or selection of a supplier in the example noted below will take place at Steps 4 and 5. However, this is not to say that there are smaller yet significant opportunities for a vendor in advance of that point. For example, a scoping project at Step 3: High Level Design, or expert input to Step 2: Complete Requirements Capture.

Fig. 5.5: Finding The Purchase Order

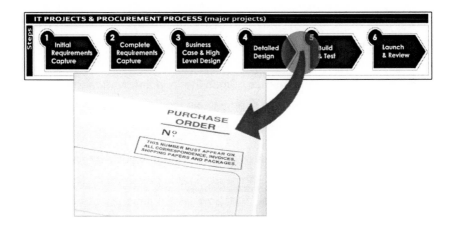

As the diagram clearly demonstrates sellers need to focus not just on the purchase order, but all those steps that surround it. Clearly the sale should not be a race to the purchase order. So, why is the purchase order so much coveted by the salesperson?

#11: PURCHASING PUSHES PAPER

Sellers have traditionally had a degree of antipathy towards purchasing departments. So too have buyers. That is because its bureaucratic ways were seen as a hindrance to the sale. However, **the role and the value of the purchasing function have been radically transformed.** Purchasing can now be a powerful ally to both buyer and seller alike.

Purchasing — The New Ally

Purchasing, once an administrative function on the periphery of the organization, now has an important strategic role. This is hardly a surprise given that purchases account for between 20% to 60% of turnover and the performance, flexibility and innovation of all the members of an organization's supply chain can have a huge bearing on its success.

Previously, purchasing was a bureaucratic department that completed transactions and managed the associated paperwork. Now it is considered to be **an integrated function**, which aims to not only make the right purchase decisions, but also choose the best suppliers and help them become even better.

IDEOLOGICAL
REVOLUTION

The Revolution Of The Purchasing Function

How the role of purchasing has changed is summarized in the table below.

TRADITIONAL PURCHASING	NEW AGE PURCHASING
• Administrative Role • A Stand-Alone Department • Vendor Management • Bureaucratic Procedures • Lowest Cost Bid • Finding The Cheapest Source • Relationships: Adversarial & Reactive • Controls Buying Decisions	• Strategic Role • An Organization-Wide Philosophy • Process For Decision Making • Best Results • Total Cost of Ownership - Value, Flexibility & Innovation • Relationships: Collaborative & Proactive • Coaches The Buying Decisions

Rather than seeking to centralize or control all buying decisions, **the new role of purchasing is to spread good buying behavior throughout the organization**. Its mission is to deliver a more sophisticated, structured and scientific approach to how purchasing decisions are made.

The new role of purchasing is to be the manager's ally and friend. It increasingly acts as a buffer to shield managers from the unwelcome attention and undue influence of vendors. Purchasing has also assumed the role of 'buying police' — protecting the organization from opportunistic vendors and bad deals.

The Ideological Revolution — Summary

As salespeople we hold certain erroneous views of how organizations buy and in particular of our power over the buying decision. Chief among them is the view that selling is the solution. This section is a reality check – selling is not the solution, the solution is getting buyers to buy. Buyers are clear on this

point - unless sellers can help buyers to buy they do not have a role to play. As this section shows new and somewhat more enlightened thinking about old problems is needed.

Having busted some of the erroneous myths that retard selling you are now ready to whole-heartedly embrace The Buying Revolution™ and profit, rather than suffer, as a result of the changes in how organizations buy. The specific opportunities to adapt your sales approach to the new realities of the marketplace are examined in **Part 2: The Sales Revolution™**.

PART II:

The Selling Revolution™

A TRANSFORMATION OF SELLING IS NEEDED

SECTION 6:

The Sales Revolution™

BUYING HAS CHANGED,
SELLING MUST FOLLOW

Introduction

The Buying Revolution™ necessitates a revolution in selling. The traditional sales strategies, techniques and skills are struggling in the face of increasingly sophisticated and spoilt-for-choice buyers.

This section outlines the future of selling and charts the revolution at each stage of the sales process, presenting 41 rules, or practical opportunities to increase win rates and sales success. It also contains real-life perspectives from buyers and sellers on what works and doesn't work in today's more competitive markets.

The Widening Gap Between Buyers And Sellers

Buyers have <u>changed how they buy</u> — the steps, the people involved and the decision-making factors are highly complex and process-driven. However, the sales approach adopted by many companies has remained the same.

Most sellers are employing the same sales tools, techniques and strategies for the past three, five or even ten years. The inevitable result is a widening gap between modern buying and traditional selling. This is illustrated in the diagram below.

Fig. 6.1 The Widening Gap Between Modern Buying & Traditional Selling

Reconciling New Buying And Traditional Selling

The Buying Revolution™ means that traditional selling is increasingly at odds with how buyers buy. Sellers have fallen behind in terms of the structure, sophistication and skill of today's buyers. Previously successful sales campaigns, sales strategies, sales processes and techniques are really struggling.

The question professional business people need to ask is: 'How do we bridge the widening gap between modern buying and traditional selling?' One thing is clear, those responsible for buying won't cross over to the seller's side and are even unlikely to meet the seller half way.

Once Successful Sales Techniques Are Struggling

In response to difficult market conditions sellers are making more sales calls, delivering more pitches and responding to more RFPs. But it is not working.

For the first time ever the sophistication of modern buying has out-paced traditional selling, as last year's cold call, sales pitch and sales proposal increasingly miss the mark.

Vendors and their well—trained sales forces, once powerful and in control, are struggling to find new customers and are increasingly being left out in the cold when major buying decisions are made.

The Ice Age For Selling

If it is The Age Of Revolution for buying, then as one sales manager quibbled it is The Ice Age for selling. That is a time when:

**PRE-SALES
REVOLUTION**

- Budgets have been frozen.
- Many salespeople have been put on ice.
- Cold calling has become the order of the day.
- There is a frosty reception for traditional vendor marketing.
- Growth ambitions are in hibernation.

So, if this is the Ice Age for selling how long will it be before the thaw sets in? How soon before a return to the good old days of customers chasing suppliers, as opposed to the other way around? Well, things won't simply return to the way that they were!

The rigor, caution and control that dominated organizational buying in the slowdown is here to stay. After all, the global slowdown has simply accelerated trends that were already underway. When it comes to the business of buying, things will never be the same again!

For those sellers who are able to adjust there are opportunities, for those that are not there are only challenges. Indeed, those species of seller unable to adjust are threatened with extension as industry roles and rules are over-turned.

The challenge for sellers is to turn the heat up on selling and to stop the freeze. As results from traditional sales methods go up in flames it is time for sellers to discover the techniques required to ignite the latent needs of their customers and unlock frozen budgets.

Sellers must re—discover what is hot in terms of sales and marketing – only this time by reference to the buyer, the buying process and the business case. In most cases that requires a revolution in selling, hence the choice of the logo, or set of icons that are used in this part of the book – the red—hot 'S'. This is the new benchmark for selling.

THE SELLING
REVOLUTION

Manifesto for the Selling Revolution™

The only response to a revolution in how organizations buy is a revolution in how they are sold to. But, how do you get revolutionary about selling? Well, by focusing on buying. In short, sellers must transform how they sell to reflect the changing needs, priorities and buying processes of buyers. It is as simple and indeed as complex as that.

The bottom line is that getting buyers to part with their money is more difficult than ever before and that reality is here to stay. Fancy sales techniques and self-serving sales processes won't do it, nor will the sales stereotype that buyers have learned to dread. Nothing short of a revolution in all aspects of selling is required.

The challenge facing today's seller is to distance him or herself from the traditional sales techniques that hinder, rather than help the sophisticated buyer to buy. Ironically the solution to getting buyers to buy is to stop selling!

Revolution At Each Stage Of The Sales Process

When we say 'in all aspects of selling' we mean at all stages of the sales process. That is from its genesis in terms of the lead to its zenith in terms of the purchase order and ultimately the repeat order. It is essential to break selling down into all its various stages as each one presents it own specific opportunities and challenges.

Let us look at the stages of the sales process in a little more detail. At its simplest the objective of selling is to generate leads and convert them through stages into orders and ultimately repeat orders. The overall rate of sales success is the sum of success at each stage of the sales process, as shown overleaf.

Table 6.1: The Stages Of The Sales Process

Stage	Title	Description	Section
1	Leads	This is the generation and management of leads from various sources.	S.7
2	Meetings	This is the first face to face encounter between buyer and seller.	S.8
3	Cycles	All those activities that run parallel to a target customer's buying process– the process of nurturing and progressing a sales opportunity.	S.9
4	Orders	This is the sales proposal, negotiation & closing – those activities aimed at winning the deal.	S.10
5	Repeat	This is the ultimate prize – the repeat sale, deepening of relationships and sales referrals.	S.11

By breaking selling down into its component parts, in this way, we are recognizing the fact that each stage of the sales process presents its own opportunities and challenges. Lead generation poses very different challenges to closing, for example. So, rather than looking for a magic bullet in terms of meeting the changed needs of buyers, we will examine the specific implications at each stage of the sales process.

The Selling Revolution™ is effectively therefore an umbrella term describing 5 different revolutions at each stage of the sales process – as shown in the diagram overleaf.

Fig. 6.1 Five Revolutions In One – The Structure Of Part Two

A revolution in selling is required in terms of how leads are generated, as well as how orders are won, and of course all stages in between. Each stage of the sales process must respond in its own way to the new requirements of today's complex buyer. Section by section we will take guidance from buyers as to the new rules that apply.

Key Opportunities And Challenges

Which stage of the sales process is most challenged by the demands of The Buying Revolution™? More important still, which of the 5 stages presents the greatest opportunities for your business? Before answering here are some questions to consider:

SALES
THE ʌLEADS
REVOLUTION

Are your traditional lead generation methods coming up short?

Buyers are facing a tsunami of cold calls and email marketing. As a result they are increasingly in hiding. Getting and keeping their attention is proving a real challenge. We address the solutions to these challenges in Section 7: The Sales Leads Revolution and use the icon of the rolodex on fire to denote the move from cold leads to warm contacts.

SALES
THE ʌMEETINGS
REVOLUTION

Are you concerned that more sales meetings are going nowhere?

Traditional sales pitches are falling on deaf ears. Buyers will turn up, but that does not mean they will open up or engage. The result is sellers are left to do all the talking while buyers keep their cards close. The future for buyer—seller encounters is discussed in Section 8: The Sales Meetings Revolution and to capture the spirit the icon of the appointment diary on fire is used.

SALES
THE ʌCYCLES
REVOLUTION

Do you often feel that, as the seller, you are on the outside looking in?

The buying process trumps the sales process every time. The seller must adopt a new role — to help the buyer to navigate their own, increasingly demanding buying process. The checklist and organizational chart on fire are the icons used in Section 9: The Sales Cycles Revolution which shows how sellers can turn the complexity of modern buying in their own favor.

SALES
THE ᴧORDERS
REVOLUTION

Are your sales proposals struggling to get projects sanctioned?

Sellers are preparing sales proposals that are of little or no value in getting projects sanctioned. After all, features and benefits don't amount to a compelling business case. The icon used is of a proposal being shredded, with closing and negotiation getting an overhaul in Section 10: The Sales Orders Revolution.

SALES
THE REPEATᴧ
REVOLUTION

Have you noticed that customer satisfaction is useless to prevent customers leaving?

Foolish notions of satisfaction fail to recognize that impact on the buyer's business is what matters. The sad reality is that few suppliers ever reach the coveted position of strategic partner. Section 11: The Repeat Sales Revolution uses the icon of the handshake and injects new life into the areas of repeat selling, account management and customer relationship management.

These questions above present some of the headline challenges of The Buying Revolution™ at each stage of the sales process, however the approach to identifying opportunities in this book is much more forensic. Each stage is addressed section by section, with seven to ten opportunities for improvement identified in each.

Upon reading this book you can choose from a total menu of more than forty opportunities to improve your sales success. Indeed, so important are these opportunities that we have elevated them to the status of 'rules' – they are the requirements of today's buyers and the future basis for competition.

The New Rules of Selling

The only truly effective sales technique is to help buyers to buy. To do this sellers must obey the rules — the new rules of selling. Based on how buyers want to be sold to, as well as on what is proving most successful for other sellers, these rules are the focus of the remainder of this book.

In total there are 41 new rules — rules which while practical, can also be demanding. However, these buyer-driven rules are already providing many sellers with a real competitive advantage. Here is a random selection of these new rules:

- Turning lead generation from a pain in the neck to a jewel in the crown
- Getting buyers to open up and engage in sales meetings
- Speaking the new language of the buyer
- Adopting the role of an expert or trusted advisor
- Accelerating the sale by facilitating the underlying buying decision
- Transforming your sales proposal into a compelling business case
- Accessing those senior managers who have the final say
- Closing more deals by helping the buyer to buy
- Developing as opposed to simply managing your existing accounts.

As sellers we don't have to like the rules. However, we cannot break the rules, they can only break us. They are at the heart of the problems faced by most sellers.

To make the new rules of selling as easy to implement as possible we have broken them down under five headings that correspond to the key stages of the sales process as discussed earlier.

You will remember that in the Introduction we set the objective of a 33% plus increase in sales based on applying the rules or principles in this book. This figure is based, not on the application of some magic bullet sales—wise, but on the achievement of a modest 3% improvement in terms of the levels of activity and effectiveness at each of the stages and more specifically from the total of more than forty opportunities, or rules listed.

Are You Ready?

Because action rather than words get results, we challenge you to adopt, over the next 30 days, the new rules of selling. That is to revolutionize all aspects of your sales process — from leads to repeat sales. In doing so, take what you find useful and leave what you do not need. Let's start at the beginning, that is the sales lead, the focus of the next section.

SECTION 7:

The Sales Leads Revolution

THE NEW RULES OF LEAD GENERATION

Why Aren't Buyers Listening?

The formula for finding new customers used to be simple. To boost sales you made more calls, sent more emails and posted more direct mail. It was a percentages game, the more pitches you threw the more homeruns you could expect to hit. How times have changed.

Lead-to-opportunity rates have hit an all time low and market conditions are only partly to blame. There is a systemic problem with respect to traditional lead generation methods that is at the core of falling campaign results.

The reality is that traditional lead generation techniques simply do not help buyers buy. They fail to provide a compelling reason for buyers to listen or to act. In fact, they make meaningful and mutually rewarding interaction more difficult, if not impossible.

Buyers no longer want to be treated like leads on a database. They don't want to be cold called, prequalified or converted. The more cold calls, email pitches and direct marketing you target towards them, the more you will witness how adept decision makers have become at avoiding your unwanted and unhelpful interruptions.

How To Turn Buyers 'OFF' Or 'ON'

Is your marketing turning buyers 'OFF' or 'ON'? Well check the table below:

How To Turn Buyers OFF:	How To Turn Buyers ON:
Cold call them.	Get introduced or referred.
Use a bought-in list.	Use permission-based marketing.
Presume they should be interested.	Ask them if it is of interest.
Pressurize them for a meeting.	Build a relationship over time.
Attempt to woo them with 'fluffy' marketing brochures.	Provide whitepapers, articles and case studies.
Read telemarketing scripts to them.	Share insights about their business and industry.

Buyers have had enough of bland and uninspiring marketing literature, telemarketing scripts and corporate websites. It is time to realize glossy brochures or bubbly salespeople full of platitudes and generalizations can no longer woo sophisticated buyers.

Buyer aversion and falling response rates mean for those that want to succeed it is time to break free from the old, discredited methods of selling and join the sales revolution. Nothing short of a complete overhaul of traditional lead generation is required.

Finding Your Next Customer

Salespeople are not only struggling to find leads, but also to convert those leads. In fact, the quantity, quality and cost of lead generation is a challenge facing over 75% of the sales managers we talk to. Yet, few appreciate the extent to which these problems are hindering their overall sales success.

There are 8 new rules that govern lead generation success. They are the remedy to struggling lead generation campaigns.

The New Rules Of Lead Generation

1. Turn up the heat on lead generation.

2. Think contacts not leads.

3. Unlock the treasure chest of contacts.

4. Conversations not campaigns.

5. Useful information not marketing blurb.

6. Get everybody involved — democratize sales.

7. Don't just look for demand, create it.

8. Get organized.

1. TURN UP THE HEAT ON LEAD GENERATION

If most organizations managed other aspects
of their business the same was as they manage lead generation they
would soon be out of business. So, it is time to turn up the heat on
lead generation.

The sad fact is some businesses seem willing to accept lead-to-meeting
conversion rates of as low as 1%, 2% or 3%. More than three-quarters
of sales managers benchmarked say the quantity, quality and cost of
lead generation is a big challenge.

While the buying revolution has accentuated the problem, lead
generation has long been the Cinderella of sales and marketing. Here
are some of the reasons why:

- **Leads are a contentious issue** in many organizations. Sellers are
  spending a disproportionate amount of time working on existing
  opportunities with little time dedicated to lead generation and
  the actual quality of leads is a bone of contention between sales
  and marketing.
- **B2B lead generation is dominated by B2C techniques.** Lead
  generation is based on mass marketing principles and
  underestimates the sophistication and specific needs of senior
  buyers.
- **Lead generation tends to be ad hoc and reactionary.** Most
  organizations do not have a target, plan or dedicated budget for
  lead generation.

The Springboard For Success

Most sales teams are content to play in the third division when it comes to lead generation even though they expect to be in the first division when it comes to selling.

The truth is many organizations are being held back because their lead generation efforts are **out of synch with their growth aspirations and strategies**. It is time managers applied the same level of sophistication to lead generation as to other aspects of selling.

The fundamental problem is that **lead generation is generally not seen as an integral part of selling**. Nor is it seen as an integral part of marketing. This is despite that for every 5% increase in the effectiveness of lead generation (i.e. more leads at existing conversion rates) you will typically witness a doubling of sales.

It is vital for sales managers to recognize that sales process improvement begins at the start of the sales process — the identification and nurturing of potential customers — and not at the end. Indeed, it is there that changes can be leveraged to achieve the greatest results. For example, sales can be increased by 400% if contacts are increased by 20% (with conversion rates being maintained).

However, to reap such rewards managers need to transform lead generation from being 'a pain in the neck' to 'a jewel in their crown'.

A System To Generate Leads

To break free from hand-to-mouth lead generation managers must look beyond simply generating more leads to creating a system to generate leads on an ongoing basis. However, for most organizations this represents a fundamental change in their approach to lead generation.

Lead Generation – The Old Vs New Way

Take the test: Which of the following words best describe your approach to lead generation? The words in the left-hand column reflect the approach adopted by 70% of the companies in our benchmarking cohort. The terms on the right describe the best practice approach to lead generation adopted by the vanguard of sales organizations.

LEAD GENERATION THAT DOESN'T WORK:	LEAD GENERATION THAT DOES WORKS:
Reactive	Proactive
Ad hoc	Systematic
Stand-alone	Integrated
Sporadic (start-stop)	Ongoing
Short term/tactical	Strategic
Mass marketing principles	Targeted direct marketing

The objective is to create an efficient and reliable means of generating leads that can create a predictable and reliable flow of potential customers consistent with the company's strategic objectives. In order to achieve this, organizations must:

- **Look beyond this quarter** and put lead generation at the centre of sales and marketing planning.
- Take a more **proactive, systematic and strategic** approach to lead generation.
- Outline a clear **target, plan and budget** for lead generation.
- Integrate **multiple sources** and adopt a campaign mindset.
- Increase the **resources allocated** to lead generation.
- Place lead generation on the agenda at sales meetings and ensure it receives **more management time and attention**.

- Develop the **right tools to help in generating leads** (e.g. replacing fluffy marketing literature with materials buyers might actually want to read).
- Clarify **the role of marketing**, with marketing being measured (in part at least) in terms of leads generated and the ability to work hand-in-hand with sales.
- Provide potential customers with a **reason to read, listen or click**. That typically requires being seen as an expert.

The problems associated with lead generation don't simply go away by themselves. Managers need to increase the sophistication of the messages, methods and systems used for lead generation if success rates are to improve.

The B2B Revolution Section 7

These are quotes from sale managers who struggle to look beyond the immediate need for leads to build a system for lead generation:

'Our approach to lead generation is ad hoc.'

'If we were developing a system to generate leads it would be very different to that which we are using today.'

'We need more leads now. We don't have the management time or resources to commit to making the change today.'

'Yes, we need to develop more effective marketing materials to use in lead generation, but we cannot wait until they are ready to begin.'

'We need to start using a sales system and to reduce our dependence on cold calling but the sales director just wants more leads, he doesn't seem to care how we get them.'

Turning Your Approach Upside-Down

So, what is **the number one key success factor** of lead generation initiatives? According to the managers we work with in the US, UK and Ireland, who are responsible for thousands of campaigns, there was almost universal agreement. The most important determinant of success is not the list or the message, nor market conditions or brand recognition. The key in determining the success of any campaign is — wait for it — realistic expectations on the part of sales managers.

Few people begin a campaign without setting goals in terms of sales meetings or revenue generated. However, the point about realistic expectations goes beyond the obvious goals set for most campaigns. When agency managers say realistic expectations are vital, what they really mean is the **expectations regarding the level of activity required and not just the results**. This is important to understand because the level of activity as an input, such as the number of phone calls, items mailed and managers spoken to, is something managers can and must actively control.

The Iceberg Principle

Managers must always remember sales success is only the tip of the iceberg. Most set targets without a full appreciation of the corresponding activity levels in terms of calls made, emails sent and contacts that will be required. Indeed, our experience suggests that 90% of campaigns underestimate the level of activity needed to ensure success.

Successful sales managers turn the 'iceberg' upside down and focus firstly on the level of activity required to achieve specific sales targets. This approach can be seen from the real world example overleaf.

There is a lot of information in the table, but it is well worth studying in more detail:

- In the example above a total of 14 people from the management team, enlisted to support the business development effort, are given the target of developing three new contacts each week.
- The target then proceeds to ensuring 20% of these new contacts result in a sales meeting and 30% of those meetings result in a sales opportunity being identified.
- Based on historic win rates the company would expect all this activity to result in new sales revenues of over $54 million.

Table 7.1: Example Of Activity-Based Approach to Targets

Bottom-Up Approach to Target-Setting 12-month period	Scenario 1	Ratio
No. of people involved in the initiative (sales team)	14	
Additional No. of contacts made/renewed per person per month	12	
Total number contacted	2016	
No. resulting in a sales meeting	403	20%
No. resulting in opportunities (buying/selling cycles)	121	30%
No. of sales opportunities resulting in a proposal/quote	36	30%
No. of quotes won	11	30%
Average order value	5,000,000	
Potential additional sales revenue generated	**54,432,000**	
Repeat	16,29,600	30%
Total	**70,761,600**	

Can you see how **deconstructing your sales target** in the manner set out above is helpful? In particular, how it draws attention to the following:

- The level of work that is required to achieve the goals set.
- The relationship between effort and result.
- The time that will be required in order for results to materialize.
- Key metrics, like conversion rates at key stages of the sales process.
- Key dependencies or risk factors.
- The longer-term commitment required to ensure success.

When it comes to appraising sales campaigns, managers focused on bottom-up targets, start conversations not by asking about results, but about the activity levels undertaken. They ask:

- How many calls have we made?
- How many contacts are being nurtured?
- How many decision makers have we spoken to?

Only after these questions have been asked is it the right time to ask about results — 'How many sales meetings have we secured and how many sales deals are we likely to close?' When managers measure activity as well as results they bring the important issues of **return on effort and effectiveness** centre stage.

Nine Deadly Prospecting Sins

So, are you ready to turn up the heat on lead generation? Are you ready to tackle the most common pitfalls? Take a look at the following list of deadly sins and ask are any of them present in your company.

1. **Sales leads appear as much by accident as by design,** leaving the company vulnerable to a slowdown in enquiries or the loss of a major customer. Where there is active prospecting it is sporadic, triggered by an imminent sales need or crisis.

2. **Salespeople regularly complain** about the shortage of leads and time spent cold calling.

3. **Poor quality leads** waste a lot of time for salespeople, with regular complaints about 'tire kickers' and a desire to only meet people who are interested and able to buy.

4. **Over-optimism regarding the potential** or immediacy of sales leads, while patchy prospect information makes accurate sales forecasting difficult.

5. **The names on prospect lists roll over** from month to month, with little cleansing of old names or elimination of cold leads.

6. **If a salesperson leaves** their prospects and leads are lost and the remaining sales staff rely on enquiries, personal contacts or some primary source of leads.

7. **An over-reliance on cold calling** and, even though the results are patchy, the burden remains with salespeople who complain about the challenge of balancing prospecting with selling.

8. **Leads are not the job of marketing**, whose discrete and sporadic activities (trade shows, ad campaigns, etc.) are isolated from prospecting.

9. **A contacts management system** is lacking or under-used, resulting in poor metrics regarding lead quality, cost and conversion rates. Some leads inevitably get lost.

2. THINK CONTACTS, NOT LEADS

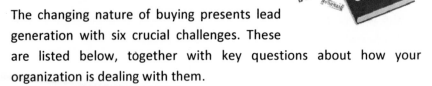

The changing nature of buying presents lead generation with six crucial challenges. These are listed below, together with key questions about how your organization is dealing with them.

(a) Being Heard Over The Noise

Buyers are being bombarded with a confusing array of similar sounding marketing messages from competing vendors. Can your efforts be heard above the 'noise' being created by your competitors?

(b) Reaching Senior Buyers

The majority of purchasing decisions rely on the approval of senior managers. However, such high-level managers are well buffered from unsolicited marketing. Is your message sufficiently compelling to get through?

(c) Providing Information Buyers Actually Need

The fact is simple — buyers place little or no value on most seller marketing. Are buyers any better off after receiving your marketing and just how useful is it to them?

(d) Influencing The Buying Process

Buyers often keep sellers at arm's length until the buying process is well underway. The result is that the seller arrives on the scene after requirements have been set and a competitive bidding situation has arisen. Can you get involved earlier in the buying cycle?

(e) Creating And Sustaining Dialogue

The ultimate test of the effectiveness of any marketing is buyer engagement. However, the response to most marketing is a deafening silence. Have you been able to create a dialogue and to get buyers to participate or respond?

(f) Generating Demand

It can be a challenge to get the attention of buyers searching for a solution. However, those already in purchasing mode are greatly outnumbered by those who do not presently have a budget or perhaps are not even aware that they have a problem. Do you have a strategy for creating demand?

The above are the reasons why thinking contacts and not leads is vitally important. The question is: Are you ready to make the transition from generating leads to developing and nurturing contacts?

It's Time To Think Contacts

Sales teams need to develop a mindset focused on mining 'contacts' rather than generating 'leads'. This represents a fundamental shift in the nature of sales prospecting, lead generation and even marketing.

Tomorrow's sales opportunities won't be generated by yesterday's lead generation techniques. Buyers are growing rapidly in sophistication and increasingly will require a process of ongoing contact and nurturing. By adopting a 'contacts' mindset companies can expect to at least double the effectiveness of their lead generation activities.

Leads Vs Contacts

You may spend money generating 'leads', but you have to invest time, energy and resources when it comes to developing 'contacts'. Before we go any further let's consider the difference between leads and contacts:

WHY LEADS ARE OUT:	WHY CONTACTS ARE IN:
Leads are generated and prequalified.	Contacts are nurtured.
Leads require a campaign.	Contacts require a conversation.
Leads are often cold.	Contacts are often warm.
Lead generation is often sporadic.	The nurturing of contacts is ongoing.
Leads are short-term in focus.	Contacts require a long-term view.
The objective is a meeting/sale.	The objective is to build a relationship/dialogue.
Leads go stale.	Contacts last forever.
Leads are found in many places.	Contacts live in a database/CRM system.

Focusing on contacts rather than leads requires the application of more contemporary, sophisticated and sustainable methods of top-filling your pipeline. It is the only sure means of managing the peaks and troughs traditionally associated with lead generation and more importantly of boosting conversion rates.

Adopting A Contacts Mindset

Changing your focus from lead generation towards building and nurturing contacts requires fundamental shifts in thinking. The following marketing communication principles are integral cornerstones for changing your organization's perspective:

- **The <u>audience</u> is wider than the sales target list.** The salesperson's black book represents only a fraction of the network of contacts that an organization must nurture.
- **The <u>objective</u> is not just to sell**, but also to start a conversation and to build a relationship. That requires a longer-term focus.
- **The <u>message</u> is not the product or the service.** It is about the business impact of the solution, together with insights into the buyer's business and industry.
- **The <u>medium</u> is a wide variety of sources**, with a focus on more buyer-friendly or 'warmer' sources. It is not just the sales and marketing department that is involved but a wider group throughout the organization — from the CFO to the project manager.
- **Nurturing contacts is <u>ongoing</u>**, compared to lead generation, which is typically campaign-based or sporadic.
- **<u>Measurement</u> is vital. A system must be used** to automate key activities (such as capturing details of online registrations or the emailing of newsletters) and track metrics in terms of activity and effectiveness.
- **<u>Organization-wide</u> participation is required**. Building and nurturing contacts will always be stifled if it is simply seen as the role of the sales team.

3. UNLOCK THE TREASURE CHEST OF CONTACTS

Most salespeople want more leads, but neglect the most promising sources available to them. They immediately turn to expensive and unpredictable methods, such as advertising, telemarketing and other forms of lead generation. At the same time they overlook the wealth of contacts scattered throughout their companies. The result is disappointment.

WHERE TO TURN FOR CONTACTS?

Customers	Counterparts in a professional body
Past Customers	Subcontractors
Referrals	Suppliers
Past employees/employers	Past proposals/enquiries
Friends and relations	Old tenders: won and lost
College mates	Industry consultants, experts and analysts
Your network	

The treasure chest of contacts is the email address books of salespeople and their colleagues company-wide. This is the ideal place to start developing a complete register of all those with whom there has been email contact. Its value derives from the fact that the majority of those contacts already know your company.

So, when was the last time your team exported all their contacts, pooled them and cross-referenced them against a defined set of target buyers?

S

Midway through the third lead generation campaign targeting major UK institutions, the sales director asked for a summary of results to date. This analysis showed a continuous slide in terms of what was being achieved. The latest campaign had barely generated a trickle of interest from the marketplace.

Reviewing the contact log of the campaign, it was clear that some hundreds of telesales calls later, direct contact had only been made with less than 20% of the target list of 250 names. It was a measure of the effectiveness of the gatekeepers and personal assistants of the various senior managers being targeted.

Searching for a better way the sales director called the management team together and enlisted their help, or more precisely their contacts. As most members of the team were industry veterans, each had contacts at different levels in most of the organizations being targeted.

By leveraging those contacts to open new doors, the company quickly rescued its sales drive from failure. As it was taking between three and five days to talk to a C level manager by means of cold calling, the director estimated that each warm contact was worth anywhere between 150 and 300 cold calls.

A Wealth Of Contacts

In most small, medium and large organizations sales systems are not used effectively. As a result a massive wealth of contacts can go unharnessed. Here are the steps involved in ensuring your organization mines its contacts effectively:

- Get team members to **export their contacts** from their email application to a spreadsheet. Ask them to organize, sort and prioritize the data in the spreadsheet based on agreed criteria regarding profile and relevance.
- Import the spreadsheet to LinkedIn, Plaxo or similar **professional networking sites** to see how far your network reaches. As a next step you can import your target list of contacts into the same professional networking site to see who you are now connected to via your extended network.
- **Combine all the spreadsheets** across the team to co-ordinate activity and allocate primary contact owners. A word of warning — you will have to do this with sensitivity and based on an agreed policy regarding how individual's contacts can be used within the organization.
- Import the individual contact spreadsheets into your sales or CRM system to create a **central repository** of contact information and to enable users to manage their contacts using the system. Ensure that the system has an administrator who will prune the data, eliminate duplication and fill any gaps. Also ensure users have full training and support in using the system and that it becomes the primary tool for sales reporting and account reviews.

4.   CONVERSATIONS,
<u>NOT</u> CAMPAIGNS

Most lead generation campaigns involve a loud and sporadic burst of marketing noise. Once these campaigns come to a close marketing silence is resumed. However, shouting at buyers is much less effective than talking with them. Bursts of cold calling, emails or direct marketing will never be enough to maximize business development over the long term.

Developing new business is the result of a sustained approach to communicating with buyers. If a salesperson wants to start a conversation with a buying unit they have to work harder than ever before. They have to adopt a systematic multi-touch approach. It is a relatively simple equation involving the number of sales calls, emails, whitepapers, case studies, letters and meetings over time.

Developing A Multi-Touch Approach

There is one golden rule when it comes to the nurturing of contacts, and that is — everything counts. Reaching and influencing buyers requires multiple methods that compliment and reinforce each other over time.

Calls   +   Emails   +   Articles   +   Letters   +   Meetings

The new rule for lead generation is to **combine multiple sources for maximum effect**. That means, for example, integrating a telemarketing initiative with a campaign landing-page on your website, the distribution of a whitepaper, a blog article, an online webinar and a public relations initiative.

Hence, instead of buyers being 'touched-off' just once, they will receive multiple complimentary 'touches' over time. If one method fails to reach or inspire the buyer, the next may succeed in its place. Every subsequent 'touch' has a similar effect to compound interest in creating and sustaining a dialogue.

Don't Expect Instant Success

This is the age of instant cash, instant downloads and instant gratification. We have been conditioned to expect an immediate response or at least a fast result. If we don't get it we believe the system is broken and we put it aside.

That mindset is a problem when it comes to sales prospecting. Hours, days and even weeks can go by before the fruits of our endeavors begin to show results. In fact, lengthening sales cycles mean the link between the lead we generate and the orders that are won can be difficult to trace.

So, **if you are looking for immediate results then look elsewhere**. Companies must look beyond this quarter and the next in terms of lead generation. They must commit to prospecting for the long haul otherwise it is a poor use of resources.

Nurturing Contacts

The problem is that traditional sales campaigns are effectively 'one trick ponies'. When the salesperson hangs up the phone or leaves the buyer's office, there is no system to ensure that future contact takes place.

Nurturing relationships must not be left to chance. This is why sales teams that continually thrive in today's difficult and dynamic marketplaces benefit from a system that helps ensure sales success.

So what does such a system look like? Well, take the following diagram as an example.

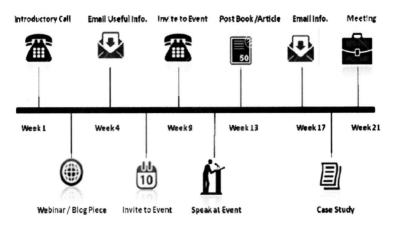

The above is an example of how the sales and marketing of an organization can be orchestrated to **nurture a prospect over time to the point of sales readiness**. It highlights ongoing contact over a 21-week period, including invitations to events and webinars, emails with useful information, case studies in the post, and so on. All this happens systematically in support of the role of the salesperson and their interaction with the prospect.

Key to enabling such an approach is the implementation of a system to manage lead generation. It cannot be done using paper-based records or business cards kept in drawers. This is something that is discussed in more detail shortly in the section It's Time to Get Organized.

'There are 82 potential customers in our largest target market. It used to be much more but we have really focused our efforts on exactly whom we need to speak to.

We have identified five key contacts within each one, giving us a total universe of 410 contacts that need to be developed and nurtured. We know we have to adopt a more integrated, multi-touch approach combining telemarketing with other activities, such as seminars, webinars and direct mail.

The question we have had to address is how much are we prepared to invest per contact in keeping this initiative going'.

Manager Financial Services Software House

Conversation Stoppers

Keeping the conversation going is essential. That requires addressing the barriers to sales campaigns becoming conversations, such as:

- **Salespeople lacking a genuine reason** to stay in touch ('I called them last month and I have nothing new to say to them.') and customers seeing no reason to welcome ongoing marketing messages from the vendor.
- **Having no system** to manage contacts. For example, triggering follow-up reminders with a contact or automating activities such as mailing email newsletters.
- **A lack of clarity** regarding who exactly should be nurtured by means of ongoing contact. This stems from the lack of a clear target market definition or target customer profile. Inevitably that leads to confusion about the prequalification criteria or overall approach.

'When we say "no" it often means "no, the timing is not right," or "no, we are not sure." Things move slowly in large organizations, so what may seem like a long time for the salesperson is not a long time in terms of the buying process. The challenge for any would-be supplier is to keep in contact so that when the timing is right they are invited to the table.'

Buyer — Major Bank

Contact Latitude

So who do you want to have a conversation with? In particular, is talking with some people a waste of time? It is important to realize, you must allow some latitude in terms of the scope of contacts to be nurtured.

Every salesperson must **be prepared to have conversations that may never go anywhere**. The key is ensuring those contacts you are talking to could, in the future, turn into customers. So salespeople must be prepared to talk to many in order to be there when the vital few eventually switch into purchasing mode.

'What surprises me is that a lot of companies do not ask for the data we have gathered during a campaign. That means all the information and intelligence that has been gathered is lost from one campaign to another. More importantly, the initial contact goes cold and it is right back to square one.'

Manager Telemarketing Agency

5. USEFUL INFORMATION, NOT MARKETING BLURB

It is time for sellers to ditch elevator scripts, bin brochures and to rewrite their web pages. Too many salespeople have started to believe their own PR even if buyers don't. Even their pitches have begun to sound like something from a marketing brochure or company press release. To engage with today's buyers it is vital to go beyond the traditional marketing hype and find some useful information to share.

No More Hype Please!

Buyers make a clear distinction between useless marketing materials and genuinely useful information. That results in a classification, such as that in the table below. Those on the right are generally considered valuable and thought provoking, while those on the left are not.

MARKETING HYPE:	USEFUL INFORMATION:
Marketing Brochures	Case Studies
Product Sheets	Whitepapers
Telesales Calls and Scripts	Information Calls
Elevator Script/Value	Analyst/Expert Reviews
Proposition	Technical Briefings
Features And Benefits List	Industry Insights/Research
Traditional Web Copy	Customer References
Press Releases	Content written by experts and
All content written by marketing	customers

The New Rules Of Engagement

If you want to engage with buyers provide them with useful information, rather than generic, inane marketing messages.

Buyers want to be rewarded when they visit your website, read your brochure or take your call. They expect to gain **some meaningful insight relevant to their business or industry**. Nine times out of ten this is not happening. Little wonder getting and keeping the attention of the buyer is such a challenge.

SELLER INSIGHT

'We knew for some time that our marketing literature was wide of the mark. It was time to replace glossy marketing brochures with whitepapers, case studies and other more useful information. But we knew, rather than being written by the people who had written our marketing material in the past, these needed to be penned by product and industry experts, as well as customers.

It cost three-times as much and took three-times longer to produce than traditional brochures. However, it was worth it. The material prompted a lot of conversations that otherwise may not have taken place, particularly with senior managers who, as we have learned, are looking beyond the technical aspects of our solution.'

CEO Global Asset Management Firm

The Product Is <u>Not</u> The Message

For years the focus has been on perfecting the sales pitch, sales presentation and call scripts. However, this has sent most salespeople in the wrong direction.

Let's take an example of the traditional cold call opening:

> 'My name is John from Astatech. We are a leading supplier of engineering solutions in the UK. We provide a comprehensive set of services in mechanical, electrical, data technologies, fire protection, interior fit-outs and facilities maintenance. I was wondering if you need help in any of these areas ...?'

How does that sound? Is that enough to get a buyer excited? No, and here is why:

- **It sounds like selling.** The caller is likely to be dispatched in a manner that befits the typical cold calling salesperson.
- **It sounds like everybody else.** It does not distinguish the seller from the hundreds of other engineering companies.
- **It's all about the seller and not the buyer.** Although it is a bit of a mouth full it does not say very much. It says nothing to the buyer in terms of the potential benefits.
- **The reaction is likely to be 'so what?'** It does not explain to the buyer why they should consider the seller's company. The buyer may already have a supplier in this area, so what reason is there to change?

Here are the rules to follow if you want to get the buyer's attention, or even get put through to the buyer, when you call:

- Give the buyer a reason to listen.
- Have something interesting to say.
- Tell stories relevant to their industry.
- Use names of other customers (ideally from the client's industry).

- Talk about the results they have achieved.
- Use terminology that is unambiguous and easily understood.
- Don't assume what you have to say is of interest. Always ask first.
- Ask if they would like to find out more.
- Above all don't try to sell on the phone.

Applying these rules to the opening of a telesales call might sound something like this:

Hello Paul,

This is Frank Byrne of Astratech calling.

We provide facilities maintenances services for A, B and C.

I just wanted to give you a quick call about some research we have just published into facilities costs in your sector and in particular key areas that have the potential to deliver savings of up to 20%.

I am not sure if this is something that would be of interest to you? But if it is, I would be delighted to provide some of the details over a coffee sometime, or email you a copy of the report.

It is vital to always remember your product, service or company is not the message. The goal should be to share stories of how the buyer's peers have solved problems relevant to your solution and offer insights regarding the opportunities and challenges facing the buyer.

6.   GET EVERYBODY INVOLVED

Organizations can no longer afford to leave selling purely in the domain of the sales department. Those companies that have expanded their business development effort **beyond the sales department** to create a 'virtual sales team' will always fair best, particularly in a difficult market.

Selling used to be the job of a few, but with the economic slowdown it quickly became apparent that **sales has to be a feature of all job descriptions**. From the CFO who leverages his contacts to get into some new accounts, the project manager who adds his contacts to the sales database or the customer support staff who revisit past customer contacts – everybody has a role.

SELLER INSIGHT

Democratizing The Prospecting Effort

'Over recent months we have effectively knocked down the walls of the sales department, getting more than 50 managers from other areas to contribute to the overall business development effort.

Whether it is two hours a week or two days a week, everybody has a part to play in the overall effort. The result has been a dramatic increase in the level of activity — one that is clearly reflecting itself in results which has helped this organization reach its monthly sales target of €1.75 million in spite of marketplace challenges.'

CEO Professional Services Firm

Your Untapped Sales Resource

In most organizations there is simply no alternative to getting everybody involved in sales. Even if it was financially possible to triple the sales team this would not present an alternative, simply because **the best people to represent your company are often your existing team** rather than a newly hired salesperson.

Our experience suggests that the success rate in hiring new sales people is only one in three or four. Even those who do make the grade can take up to nine months before they are effective. So, hiring new salespeople is not necessarily the solution.

Moreover, buyers prefer dealing with experts and not salespeople. In the world of complex B2B sales your team's knowledge of not only its products, but of the customer's industry is key to sales success. This is the vital X Factor that a new sales hire won't have.

Breaking The Barriers

While it is vital to expand sales beyond the sales team, it can present challenges. The secret to success is to address all these challenges up front.

'In a difficult market it is all hands to the pump,' one CEO told his staff recently. When he encountered resistance he spoke directly — 'There are lots of reasons why this won't work, but only one reason why it cannot fail – that reason is survival.'

Getting people to contribute to the task of nurturing their contacts and contributing to the sales effort will require the following ingredients:

- An investment in tools, skills and one-to-one support.
- Leadership from the top, together with ongoing coaching, encouragement and support to all those involved.

- Putting business development on the agenda at all management and team meetings.
- Co-ordination across the team — that is a plan, a process of review and a central repository of contact information.
- A special effort in order to sustain the initiative beyond the initial spurt of effort.
- A system for reporting activities undertaken and results achieved.
- Overcoming sensitivities with respect to the sharing of contact information throughout the organization.
- Issuing a policy statement regarding how shared contacts will be used.
- A budget for the initiative, including more client meetings, the attendance at more industry events, client entertainment and so on.

SELLER INSIGHT

We Don't Want To Turn You Into Salespeople

'We don't want to turn you into salespeople,' declared the company CEO to the assembled group of partners, division heads and managers. 'After all, the last thing our customers want is to see another salesperson!' he added with a laugh.

'However, to maintain our growth we need you to share your expertise and insight with potential customers. We need you to tell more people about the projects, the awards and the skills of our company.

'Since launching the initiative to expand the sales effort, sales activity is up by 900% and revenues, previously sliding through the floor, have increased with month-on-month targets achieved.'

Manager Engineering Services Firm

7. DON'T JUST LOOK FOR DEMAND, CREATE IT!

In times of buoyant demand lead generation focuses on identifying and selling to those with both a need and a budget. However, sales teams that are successful over the long-term develop strong relationships with their contacts to ensure that if and when a need arises they are there to supply the solution.

Tapping Latent Market Demand

For every prospect in buying mode today, there are at least four that are not. Remember, those not interested in buying today could be the customers of tomorrow. The new role of lead generation is to tap into and exploit this latent demand.

Of course, salespeople cannot create demand by themselves. Every salesperson needs the back up and support of marketing. Indeed, the notion of creating, as well as finding demand is at the core of this new approach to lead generation.

Generating Demand

Sales teams cannot reliably meet their targets by simply selling to those who are ready to buy. For every customer shopping for a solution there are others that don't realize they have a problem or a budget to resolve it.

A clear focus on demand generation is one of the most fundamental elements that will help unlock these 'dormant' opportunities. However, to achieve this the skill set of the salesperson must evolve.

Demand generation requires:

- **New levels of confidence, knowledge and skill.** The salesperson must be able to connect with the customer's business and industry drivers to shape the business case.
- **A mindset change.** The focus has to be on activities that may not contribute to this year's target. The payback from demand generation activities, while difficult to measure, is long term. So it requires a commitment of time and resources to activities that may not payback this quarter or perhaps this year.
- **New approaches to prequalification.** Instead of concentrating on prequalification, the emphasis needs to switch to marketing and nurturing. Contacts need to be nurtured to sales readiness on an ongoing basis. It means replacing budget, authority, timing and need as the criteria for whom to target, with profiling customers based on the basis of sector, size and so on. Prequalification is not scrapped, but is held off until a sales cycle is nascent.
- **New metrics and a longer term horizon.** The philosophy of demand generation runs counter to the existing metrics and incentives used by managers and their teams. Compared to selling to those actively searching for a solution, it could triple the time from first meeting to sale, while also dramatically cutting conversion rates.
- **Marketing and sales working well together.** But the marketing required is not that of the glossy brochure. Rather it centers on providing useful, relevant and credible information to the buyer (e.g. whitepapers, case studies, etc.).
- **Deep pockets.** Educating the market and generating awareness is expensive, particularly for smaller companies. It would be much easier to wait for competitors to generate demand in the market and then exploit it. Alas, however, waiting for somebody else to do it is often not an option.

How Can You Create Demand?

As a first step in creating demand, sellers must decide what fundamental needs exist in the target market (business drivers, priorities, strategies, events, and so) that can be leveraged to generate demand. Here are two good examples we came across recently:

- A supply chain solutions supplier recently took advantage of a food safety scare to highlight how their solution could help radically reduce the costs associated with meeting food traceability regulations.
- An IT supplier surveyed its top customers to discover their priorities for next year. With security, cost and compliance emerging as key, the company wrote a series of best practice guides in each area and organized seminars to heighten awareness of these challenges and generate demand for its solutions as a result.

Of course, fundamentally a basic need has to exist, such as the desire to cut costs, save time or ensure compliance. As professional sales and marketing people the challenge is to show how the performance of the buyer's business can be improved in a compelling way. As in all aspects of sales and marketing, it is crucial to focus demand generation efforts on the right customer and the most appropriate solution.

10 Steps To Generating Demand

If salespeople wait until buyers are in 'shopping mode' they are likely to arrive **too late to shape the buying decision**. They are also more likely to be drawn into a competitive bidding situation. To avoid this happening here are 10 steps to follow:

1. Help buyers to evaluate and reassess their **priorities** by comparing them with their counterparts and peers.

2. Quantify the threats and opportunities relating to their industry using independent **experts** to enhance credibility.

3. Show them the results achieved by their **peers** with your solutions.

4. Provide **useful information** not marketing blurb.

5. Talk to the **senior managers** who shape priorities, allocate budgets and make decisions.

6. Run **educational events**, such as talks, seminars and webinars, where customers and experts can talk about industry challenges and how they can be resolved.

7. Position your company as a **thought leader**. For example, by writing articles, sponsoring research or speaking at events you can provoke and compel buyers to sit up and take notice.

8. Link your solution with a **campaign or cause** that already has momentum. It can be easier to rally people around a cause than a product or service.

`9. Enlist the support of others in generating demand, such as **industry associations** and experts.

10. It is important to note that effective demand generation is not just one activity, but a program of activities. To be effective it must be **sustained over time**.

These tips may seem like common sense, however 67% of the firms we have benchmarked this year are adopting less than four of these 10 steps.

By adopting the 10 steps above sellers can help buyers to understand and appreciate their needs. That means they are 'there when the light goes on' and the search for a solution and a supplier begins.

Avoid Prequalification Pitfalls

Sales teams have to spread their nets wider. They can no longer just rely on engaging with just those that meet traditional BANT (Budget, Authority, Need and Timing) prequalification criteria. They also need to seek companies that offer longer-term potential. This means companies need to replace the over-prequalification of leads with nurturing and marketing.

Different Levels Of Prequalification

A salesperson's time is precious and they should only meet with those buyers that are relevant and appropriate. However, many sellers are guilty of over zealously prequalifying leads, often screening out companies that cannot buy now but could buy in the future.

Rigorous prequalification of sales opportunities is an obvious must. However, the level of prequalification necessary for leads should not be as vigorous as the prequalification used to underpin the probability ratings in your sales pipeline.

So what is the difference between the old criteria for prequalification and the new method of nurturing contacts? Well the table overleaf makes this clear.

OLD PRE-QUALIFICATION QUESTIONS:	NEW PRE-QUALIFICATION QUESTIONS:
Is there a budget available? Does the manager have the authority to buy? Is the timing right? Do they need the solution now? The KEY question used to be: 'Will they buy?'	Does the company fit our predefined profile? Might they have a need? Could they buy? Is there potential fit for our solution? Do we have access to senior management? The KEY question now is: 'Should we talk?"

From Target Lists To Target Customer Profiles

One reason why pre-qualification is over-used is because companies are directing their sales and marketing efforts at:

- Confused target market profiles.
- Broad marketing lists that are often of poor quality.
- Marketing databases that are in need of pruning.
- Large markets without specific target customer profiles.

In these cases the only way to compensate for the low quality of the list or database is through prequalification. But why prequalify companies that should not be the subject of your sales and marketing in the first place? Why use prequalification in place of careful targeting and screening?

Nurture Instead Of Prequalifying

If you have precisely targeted your marketing you should have the confidence to leave the prequalification to the buyers. After all, it is they that will decide what companies they will speak to and when.

Your focus should be on providing the buyer with **a compelling reason to listen, meet and talk**, as well as a reason to buy. This assumes the buyer has been carefully chosen to fit the profile of companies that may potentially require the supplier's solution.

The big problem right now is when companies say they are not interested, salespeople simply move on. However, for companies that fit your target profile it is important to commit to developing and nurturing contact over the long haul, even if today they are saying 'no'. This involves applying the model shown in the earlier rule called 'Think Conversations, Not Campaigns'.

The key to enabling such an approach is the implementation of a system to manage lead generation. It cannot be done using paper-based records or business cards kept in drawers.

SELLER INSIGHT

'The days of buying a list and then hitting the phones to find the next customer are over. I am convinced of two things: you cannot buy a good list and cold calling is dead. After all, what have we got to show for hundreds of calls made? Well, almost nothing. Between voicemail, no-names policies and gatekeepers the chances of even getting to talk to a manager, especially a senior one, are abysmally low. There has to be a better way.'

Sales Director in a Growing Technology Company

8. TIME TO GET ORGANIZED

Lead generation has fallen behind almost every other aspect of sales and marketing in terms of the level of sophistication, structure and indeed discipline applied.

The result is that many organizations are experiencing a hand-to-mouth existence in respect of lead generation. The solution to this quandary requires looking beyond the salesperson to the systems, structures and processes of the organization in respect of lead generation.

Lead generation will continue to struggle unless it is put on an entirely new footing. That requires managers to look beyond issues such as the amount of time salespeople spend cold calling or the next sales campaign, to lead generation as a core competence of the organization. It is time for a more scientific approach to lead generation.

Where Is The Plan?

Marketing campaigns traditionally have tended to focus heavily on the creative, rather than the scientific. This is at the root of the challenges facing lead generation.

Preparing a plan, target and budget for lead generation is the key to transforming lead generation from an art to a science. It requires answering the following questions before any more money is spent on lead generation:

- What <u>campaigns</u> will be run throughout the year?
  - How will different campaigns be knitted together?
  - What is the best timing?
- What <u>sources</u> of contacts will be used?
  - How will the various sources used be integrated?
- What <u>messages</u> will be delivered?
  - How will they resonate with the issues, priorities and events of relevance to prospects?
- What is the ideal <u>target customer profile</u>, including markets or segments?
  - What is the <u>criterion</u> for 'a good lead'?
  - What level of prequalification is appropriate?
- When is a lead 'sales ready'?
  - What is the <u>process for nurturing</u> those that are not ready to see a salesperson yet?
- What is the <u>budget</u>? How will it be allocated (cost of the various sources, marketing materials, etc)? What return will it generate?
  - How and when will the progress of lead generation be <u>reviewed</u>?
  - What <u>metrics</u> will be used to measure success (conversion rates, etc)?
- What are the <u>key actions</u> required to deliver on the plan? When are they to be completed? Who is responsible?
  - What <u>systems</u> will be used to support the program of lead generation (e.g. sales database or contact management system)?

Where Is The System?

In many companies the level of **administrative efficiency with respect to leads** is poor, as evidenced by:

- A multiplicity of lists, notes and records across users and departments.
- Sales systems only being used by a limited number of salespeople and with minimal data management and pruning.
- The manual handling of leads that could be automatically captured from the web, for example.

The consequences are:

- An inevitable duplication of effort, as well as poor follow-up and follow-through.
- Some leads going 'cold' or falling 'through the cracks'.
- Contact management being left to chance.

The core of this problem is the fact that most organizations do not have an **effective database or CRM system to sort, track and manage leads**. Those that do often struggle to ensure it is fully used by salespeople.

Based on our benchmarking of sales organizations, employing a sales system can boost the effectiveness of lead generation by up to 35%. There is of course a price to be paid for this efficiency — the challenges of implementation and adoption of such systems is generally well in excess of what managers expect.

However, once you have properly planned and targeted your lead generation activities and implemented a system to nurture these contacts, you will have built the foundation necessary to reinvigorate your success.

The Sales Leads Revolution — Summary

Buyer aversion and falling response rates to lead generation approaches means it is time to break free from the old, discredited methods of lead generation. There are eight key principles that will reinvigorate your success rate when it comes to discovering potential clients.

1. **Turn up the heat on lead generation**. The challenge is to apply the same level of sophistication and rigor to lead generation as to other aspects of selling.

2. **Think contacts not leads**. The term 'leads' is troublesome and out-dated. 'Leads' are out and 'contacts' are in and the focus must shift to developing and nurturing contacts.

3. **Unlock the treasure chest of contacts**. Remember the single richest source of contacts is you, your network, your colleague's network, your email address book and the stack of business cards that have been gathered over the years.

4. **Think conversations not campaigns**. Forget stop-start sales campaigns. Sales teams need to commit to prospecting for the long haul. They must look beyond this quarter.

5. **Useful information not marketing blurb**. Buyers are tired of marketing speak, so it is time to ditch the hype and instead to share stories/insights of how the buyer's peers have solved problems, or exploited opportunities.

6. **Get everybody involved.** It is time to democratize sales. Selling is no longer just up to the sales team, it is a team sport that everyone - from the CFO to the project manger - must contribute to.

7. **Don't just look for demand, create it.** If salespeople wait until buyers are in 'shopping mode', they will most likely arrive too late to shape the buying decision. Thus, it is important to market to those who do not yet have a budget, or have latent needs. In this way salespeople are front of mind when the 'light goes on' and the need is realized.

8. **Get organized**. Sales managers need to look beyond the salesperson to the systems, structures, plans and processes required to top fill the pipeline with leads.

The eight steps above will help you present the compelling reason for a contact to read, listen or click and ultimately to meet with you. Having secured the meeting let's turn to the challenge of making it successful. That is the focus of the next section – Section 8: The Sales Meeting Revolution.

SECTION 8:

SALES
THE ∧MEETINGS
REVOLUTION

The Sales Meeting Revolution

THE NEW RULES FOR SALES MEETINGS

The undeniable fact is that buyers are meeting fewer salespeople. Even if salespeople are granted access they are often not meeting the right people — the decision-makers who have tight control over purchasing budgets.

Little wonder then that most sales managers share one major complaint — their sales teams are not meeting enough new prospects. They also are left wondering why many of the meetings that do take place fail to progress further.

Managers are quickly realizing that the traditional means used by their sales teams are proving ineffective in the face of increasingly difficult to impress buyers.

Let's take the typical scenario. The salesperson arrives determined to sell and delivers a well-rehearsed presentation. However, the potential customer gives little away and the salesperson is left to do most of the talking. After the meeting, despite a few follow-up emails and phone calls, any initial interest seems to evaporate and things quickly stall.

To change this all too familiar pattern sales managers need to radically overhaul their team's approach to sales meetings if they want to improve their success rate at capturing new business.

Why Sales Pitches Don't Work

Sales managers often focus on revamping sales pitches, rehearsing answers to objections and improving preparations and prequalification. However, improving your pitch, presentation and preparation is futile. These are no longer key when it comes to successfully engaging with buyers.

The New Rules Of Sales Meetings

If sales teams are to succeed where they are currently failing, managers must help their sales teams embrace the new rules of sales meeting success:

1. Revise Your Objectives.

2. Slow Down, Stop Selling.

3. Have Conversations, Not Presentations.

4. Listen, Before Talking.

5. Deliver Insights, Not Information.

6. Be An Expert, Not A Salesperson.

7. Make It Easy To Say 'No'.

8. Make Time For Preparation.

9. Keep In Touch.

1. REVISE YOUR OBJECTIVES

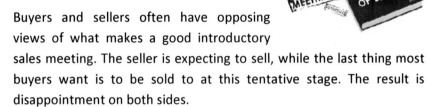

Buyers and sellers often have opposing views of what makes a good introductory sales meeting. The seller is expecting to sell, while the last thing most buyers want is to be sold to at this tentative stage. The result is disappointment on both sides.

Don't Make False Assumptions

We have asked many sales professionals what they want to achieve when meeting a prospective client. Here is a sample of their typical responses:

- To identify the client's needs and requirements.
- To communicate the advantages of the solution they are selling.
- To prequalify the opportunity.
- To tell the client about their company.
- To establish rapport.
- To make a sale.

These responses highlight the **six erroneous assumptions** made by salespeople regarding the initial sales meeting:

1. **The buyer has prepared** in advance of the meeting and, of course, remembers exactly what it is about.

2. **The buyer is ready to buy** and wants to be sold to. They want to learn about the seller's company and its products. They have already identified a need and have set aside a budget.

3. **The buyer will immediately open up and engage**.

4. **Taking control is the best way** to run a sales meeting. That includes setting the agenda and doing most of the talking.

5. **A well-rehearsed pitch or presentation** is the most effective way to communicate information.

6. **'Naturally gifted salespeople' are almost effortlessly good** in sales meetings — their personality, charm and communication skills will see them through.

These falsehoods are at the heart of why most sales meetings don't progress as expected and why buyers are meeting fewer salespeople than ever before.

Understanding The Objectives

Salespeople sometimes make the mistake of thinking just because they have travelled to the meeting the buyer owes them their attention, engagement and a possible next step. However, most buyers don't see it the same way.

When a buyer agrees to meet a salesperson they have done their fair share. After all they have:

- Taken the risk of exposing themselves to 'another salesperson'.
- Given you some of their scarce time.
- Shared with you some information about their company.
- Given you their email address, mobile or direct-line number.
- Taken you inside their company and perhaps introduced you to colleagues.

So, just what are you giving them in return? A sales presentation or sales pitch? The simple truth is, buyers are generally poorly rewarded for the time they spend in sales meetings.

The Real Purpose of Meeting

Salespeople need to drop their own agenda and focus instead on the buyer in their sales meetings. When buyers agree to meet with a salesperson for the first time they want to explore, rather than to be sold to. The purpose from the salesperson's perspective should therefore be to:

- Share insights and other valuable information.
- Understand the needs and priorities of the buyer.
- Determine if they can provide a valuable solution.
- Help the buyer.
- Assess the level of interest and discover if 'we should be talking.'

By embracing the above principles, not only do buyer and seller meet, but they also engage. The result is that they are likely to meet again and are far more likely to advance in the direction of a sale (if an opportunity for one exists).

Sales Meeting Sins

When you get the purpose of the sales meeting wrong, you are likely to commit one or more of the following sins:

1. Delivering a sales pitch when you should be sharing useful information.

2. Giving a sales presentation when you should be having a conversation.

3. Listing product information when you should be sharing valuable industry insights.

4. Telling a client, 'You need this!' when you should be asking, 'Is this of any interest?'

5. Talking at length about your company when you should be listening to understand about their company.

6. Pushing a solution when you should be exploring their needs?

7. Selling, when you should be focused on helping the buyer.

Starting The Conversation

It is rare for buyers to engage fully in the first meeting. Increasingly, they are adopting a 'wait and see' approach to their encounters with salespeople.

So, today's successful first meeting is not a sales pitch or presentation, and should not involve a slick sales technique. None of these things help the buyer to buy. Getting the post-revolution buyer to engage requires a very different approach.

Should We Be Talking?

The objective of the initial sales meeting encounter is to answer one question and one question only. That is — 'Should we be talking?' In other words: 'Is our solution and what we have done for others of interest to your company?', 'Would you like to explore it further at this time?' and 'Is this something that is now or could be in the future a priority for your business?' As salespeople we need to remember that the initial brief encounter is not to do all the talking there and then, but to decide if both parties should be talking now.

Before you race off to your next sales meeting, ask yourself if you are a 100% confident about the type of meeting the buyer expects will take place? Is it a presentation? Is a formal pitch expected? Is there going to be a group present?

Revise The Agenda

Before every sales meeting it is vital to talk to the buyer about what they want to achieve and who will be attending the meeting. You'd be surprised at the number of salespeople we meet who admit to being surprised when walking into a meeting and discovering there are five people waiting to see them rather than the one person they expected.

Salespeople always have to put the buyer's agenda ahead of their own. They have to place the buyer in the driving seat. The salesperson's job is to clearly set the meeting expectations and help coach and support buyers through the appropriate next steps. We will discuss this in more detail later.

2. SLOW DOWN, STOP SELLING

Even though salespeople are under increased pressure to sell, the introductory meeting is definitely not the place to do it. To increase your chances of progressing to a sales cycle, leave the selling for another day.

Most salespeople try to achieve too much in their first meeting with a buyer. They go flat out selling while presenting product and company information, eliciting needs, presenting a solution and answering objections. All this in somewhere between 30 and 50 minutes.

Based on our experiences sales teams are selling too fast and too soon. They look to present a solution without a sufficient understanding of the buyer's requirements. The salesperson must resist the temptation to propose solutions in the first meeting. In most cases doing so will hinder rather than advance the complex sale.

Don't Be Tempted To Sell Prematurely

Sometimes the salesperson could be forgiven for assuming the buyer wants to be sold to. Often buyers can ask questions that will tempt the salesperson into sales mode far too early in the process. However, it is vital not to get lured into trying to sell too early. Overleaf are some questions buyers may ask in the first meeting and how you can avoid falling into the trap of delivering the wrong answer.

Question: 'Why should we pick you?'

> Old Answer: 'Well, we are the industry leader. We have won several industry awards. Our technology is the most feature-rich. We have been in business for more than 10 years.'

New Answer: 'Well, to be honest, I would like to learn more about your requirements in order to be able to answer that question properly. Having said that, companies like Acme 1 have picked us because of our specialized industry knowledge, while companies like Acme 2 have picked us because we can meet their unique support requirements. If we could chat a bit more about your requirements, I will be able to better understand if we are the best fit for your company at this time.'

So, which do you prefer? Well, the old answer draws the salesperson into selling too soon, before the conversation has really begun. It also sounds like a stereotypical salesperson — something that we are equally anxious to avoid.

Here are another two examples:

Question: 'So how much is this going to cost?'

Old Answer: 'I can put together a quotation for you. It depends on your budget and requirements. What had you planned to spend?'
New Answer: 'Well, I would need some more information to be able to give you specifics as regards price. However, I can talk about other projects, their scope and their cost. For example...'

Question: 'I am sorry but I only have 30 minutes. Tell me a bit about your services?'

Old Approach: 'Sure. We were established in 1999. There are 220 people in the company today. We have an office in London and in Dublin. There are three parts to our business...'
New Approach: 'I'd be happy to John. We have helped several companies similar to yours address various problems, with each one having slightly different priorities. I have a number of references I can talk you through. As we only have 25 minutes is there any particular area that you would like me to focus in on?'

Selling Prevents Engagement

The faster a salesperson is to sell in an initial meeting, the slower the buyer will be to engage. The buyer may sit back patiently as the salesperson delivers their presentation, but is unlikely to be truly engaged.

Buyers are often happy to let the salesperson do all the talking, while keeping their own cards held close. The result is many sales meetings end without the salesperson understanding if there is any real interest or even a valid opportunity. Worst of all they leave without knowing what the appropriate next step should be.

'Stop selling' may certainly sound like strange advice, but the reality is that most salespeople perform at their best when they stop selling. When the pressure to sell is removed salespeople begin to listen more closely to their customers' needs and in turn decision makers start to open up about what they need and want. As a result the chances of success are vastly increased.

'Several times a month we receive the standard text reminder, "Always be closing." This is a theme followed through in every sales meeting, where the same manager, repeats the line "the only difference between losing and closing is a 'C'." However, I know that if I applied that logic in my meetings with buyers I would get absolutely nowhere.

I make a point of honestly telling all those that I meet, that whether they spend €150,000, €50,000 or nothing, I am not there to sell to them, but rather to help. And I do mean it. I tell them about what other customers are doing and listen to what they want to achieve and we take it from there. It will take several meetings, but my success rate is the best of my team.'

European Corporate Advertising Agency Manage

3. CONVERSATIONS, NOT PRESENTATIONS

It is time to ban sales pitches and presentations from early stage meetings. Buyers want to have interesting and insightful conversations, not sales meetings with even fancier sales presentations.

Dialogue Rather Than Monologue

The real test for any salesperson is to get the buyer to engage. But most sales pitches and presentations are based on delivering a monologue as opposed to building a dialogue between buyer and seller.

The PowerPoint presentation is the salesperson's worst enemy. Formal sales presentations obviously play a role in the sales cycle, but not at such an early stage.

The first sales meeting should be a two-way exchange of ideas, and a joint exploration of problems and their solutions. In this context, when presentations are given their content requires great care. Always remember that at this stage the presentation is not the main event, it is merely the sideshow.

The least effective way to conduct your meetings is to use the traditional 'face-off' scenario where you sit across from the buyer and make a presentation. **The most effective sales meetings are not actually sales meetings at all.** They are conversations.

The same rules that apply to presentations also apply to demonstrations undertaken at a first meeting. Presenting a demo before the customer's business drivers, product requirements and background are established is often a mistake. Most demos tend to focus on features, as opposed to benefits, and rarely illuminate the issue of business impact or results.

If at all possible hold back a demo until it can have greatest impact in the sales cycle. However, inevitably sellers face situations where they will be specifically asked to produce a demo and they will have no choice but to comply, failure to do so would result in disqualification from the buyer's process. In these cases it is critical to set the expectation that the demo will only give an indication of capability and that once the client's needs are fully understood a tailored demonstration will be put together that more accurately reflects their exact requirements.

Never Start with A Sales Pitch

Over the years buyers like salespeople have been conditioned. When they walk into a sales meeting they are expecting a slide show and a sales pitch.

So, what do you do when the prospect asks you to start the meeting by telling them about your company? Well, some books recommend you reply — 'I would love to and there are lots of interesting things to tell, but in order for me to understand what areas I should focus on, I would like to learn a little about your company first.'

Now, in principle that makes sense. However, we find buyers often want to hear a little from the seller before they engage. By starting off with a short introduction you give your prospect a little more comfort, as well as the chance to focus on what the meeting is about. This is important because you cannot assume the prospect has done any preparation in advance of the meeting.

With this in mind we recommend having a short overview of your company that will grab attention and set a direction for the conversation. For example:

'We have helped other companies in your industry. We helped Acme 1
and Acme 2, for example, cut the cost of complying with regulatory
compliance by up to 35% by providing new technology to make
reporting simpler.

In the process we have noticed some interesting trends with respect to
the processes and technologies being deployed and in particular where
additional savings can be gained.

I am delighted to have the opportunity to discuss this with you for 45
minutes and see if it is something that is relevant to your business.

While I am going along I can explain a little about our company and
leave you with some material.

Does that make sense or is there something else that we should cover in
particular? I was thinking it would take 45 minutes. Is that ok? '

This is a lot better than a long-winded 'about us' monologue or
product pitch. It indicates to the buyer that you have some useful
insights to share, that you are not just there to sell and that you are no
ordinary salesperson.

Notice what is happening here:

- By mentioning the names of other companies you add credibility
  to your message.
- By confirming the topic to be discussed and the time available,
  you manage expectations and demonstrate you are respectful
  of the buyer's time.

Engaging with the buyer in a conversation is the real test of the
salesperson. If the buyer is not saying very much then take care. Read
the signals — ask if this is of interest and be prepared to go back to
square one to find out what is.

10 Conversation Stoppers

Some conversations between buyer and seller never really take off, but to prevent this happening make sure you avoid:

1. PowerPoint Presentations.

2. Talking too much about yourself/company while failing to listen.

3. Failing to show a genuine interest in the buyer and his business.

4. Asking too many or inappropriate questions.

5. Telling stories that suggest breach of confidence.

6. Talking negatively about the competition.

7. Running over on time.

8. Evading questions or fluffing answers.

9. Making what appear to be exaggerated claims.

10. Looking for a big commitment from the buyer too soon.

Why Are Buyers Slow To Open Up?

Past experience with salespeople has made buyers very cautious. They have become highly skeptical and eager not to make any early commitments especially when high-impact, high-value purchase decisions need to be made. In meetings they can appear withdrawn and disinterested.

In fact, while the salesperson is enthusiastically making his PowerPoint presentation or talking about his solution the buyer is usually thinking:

- Where is the proof to back-up these claims?
- Who else uses this solution in our industry and what results have they achieved?
- Could I really work with this person?
- I have heard all this before.

- This is a typical salesperson. I don't want to be prequalified or closed.
- You don't seem to know much about my industry or business.
- I have another meeting to go to. How do I get out of this?

Because purchases now tend to have larger strategic implications, managers involved in championing a specific purchase or supplier will have their decision scrutinized from many different levels within the organization. Therefore, buyers are even more circumspect when dealing with suppliers looking to sell.

To overcome these challengers salespeople must focus on building trust. And the only way to build trust with a buyer is by developing a genuine understanding of their perspective. The simple secret of achieving this means you have to focus on doing one thing — listening.

4. LISTEN, BEFORE TALKING

Listening is essential in sales. When sales deals turn sour it is usually because the salespeople involved were not listening to what the buyers were telling them or they were misinterpreting what the buyer was saying.

Your primary goal as a salesperson should be to listen carefully, to learn about and understand the prospect's problems so that you can sell your solutions.

By asking questions and listening to the prospect you build awareness of the problem, as well as ownership of the solution. These are two vital ingredients of your sales success.

BUYER INSIGHT

'The Executive Suite can be a lonely place. If we trust the salesperson and feel they will listen, we tend to open up.'

Senior Manager — Buyer, Multinational Corporation

The Listening Challenge

Contrary to popular opinion great salespeople are not great talkers, but great communicators. The key difference is the ability to listen.

The eternal debate in selling surrounds the proportion of time the salesperson should spend talking, as opposed to listening. Is it 70:30 or 50:50 in favor of the salesperson? Does the ratio change over the course of the sales cycle, with the buyer expected to do more talking at the earlier stages?

One thing is clear you cannot arrive at a sales meeting and expect to ask lots of questions and spend your time listening. On the other hand, you absolutely cannot spend most of the time talking. There is a delicate balance to be struck.

The rule must simply be to start a conversation that genuinely engages the buyer. Again the magical words are 'conversation' and engagement — thinking this way naturally ensures the right balance of listening and talking.

10 Tips To Improve Your Listening

Listening, unlike talking, often does not come naturally to salespeople. It requires study and practice. So, here are some tips that can help:

1. **You must earn the right to listen** and encourage the prospect to open up, by showing that you are credible, trustworthy and attentive. You must also tell the prospect that you want to listen and why. For many buyers this may seem unusual or even unwelcome. Salespeople are often expected to talk rather than listen, but it is time to break the mould.

2. **Listening is an attitude**. It is built on openness and respect for the person talking. To listen well you need to be genuinely interested in the other person and what they have to say.

3. **Listening is active, not passive**. It is a full body activity. It requires giving back visual encouragement to the speaker (face the speaker, maintain eye contact, nod your head as you listen, etc).

4. **Listening requires patience and discipline**. Resisting the temptation to interrupt or to jump in is crucial. Your challenge is to let the speaker tell their story in their own words and at their own pace.

5. **Great communicators empathize**. They also understand the emotional context by reading the language being used, as well

as the emotions and the body language of the person talking. Reading the buyer's signals is a key part of listening.

6. **Beware of making judgments.** You need to remain objective and open-minded. This is important because what the buyer is saying is often overlaid with our own internal chatter — a silent running commentary so to speak. To really connect with the person talking it is important to sweep away your preconceived notions and engage with what is being said.

7. **Probe by asking open questions.** By asking open-ended questions such as, 'How do you feel about that?' you can explore the wider implications of what is being said.

8. **Take some notes.** This will aid your concentration at the time and assist your recall after the event. It can also demonstrate that you are listening. This sounds pretty obvious but our experience suggests that one in four salespeople fail to take notes in customer meetings. But always be careful not to let your note taking put the buyer off.

9. **Check regularly to ensure you understand** what is being said. You should confirm your understanding of key points.

10. **Keep your ego in check.** Remember it is not about you — it is about the buyer. Resist the temptation to show that you know more than the buyer and protect the prospect's ego at every turn. Remember listening is also a manifestation of confidence on the part of the listener, so listen without interrupting.

5. INSIGHTS, NOT INFORMATION

Buyers are not interested in your company and your product. They are only interested in how you can benefit their business. You need to communicate compelling stories of how customers have benefited from your solution and how industries are changing.

The Killer Sales Pitch

Do you have a killer sales pitch? Have you developed one knock out combination of words to communicate the greatness of your solution and make your customers salivate? Probably not, few sellers have.

So, why is the 'killer sales pitch' so hard to find? Well, because salespeople are looking in the wrong place. They are looking to their brochures, catalogues and press releases for the answer. Yet, it cannot be found in lists of features and benefits, elevator pitches or sales presentations.

The reason why salespeople struggle with their message is because the killer sales pitch isn't a pitch — it is an insight! It is not the explanation of 'why we are so great', but rather the answer to 'why you should care'. In short, the perfect sales pitch has to be preceded with 'here is something useful you should know.' Remember, the insights must motivate action and engagement.

Sharing Insights

The salesperson can no longer simply act like a talking brochure. Buyers want something more than marketing blurb and techno babble in return for the time they invest in a meeting. They want to be told something that:

- Is interesting and topical.

- Is relevant to their company and its industry.

- Reflects in at least some way their strategic priorities.

- Recounts the experience of peers.

- Is relevant to the performance of their business.

- Shows the seller has invested some time thinking about the buyer's business.

Setting A New Agenda

Our benchmarking data shows that seven out of ten salespeople set meeting agendas that limit the conversation, as well as the interaction with the buyer – they are focused on the left-hand-side of the table below.

SELLER-FOCUSED AGENDA	BUYER-FOCUSED AGENDA
• Introductions • Our company • Our products & services • Our clients • Our strengths • Proposed next steps	• Insights: opportunities/challenges • The results you want to achieve • The results achieved by other customers • Your needs and requirements • How to explore this further and ways to proceed

So, to ensure you optimize the chances of your first meeting with a prospective client rewrite the agenda to make it buyer-focused.

Setting Meeting Expectations

Too often salespeople go to meetings expecting to sell, while at the same time buyers arrive expecting to be sold to. These old habits and expectations can be hard to change. In most cases however, nobody will have actually clarified what exactly the objective of the meeting is and what it will cover.

It may seem obvious to suggest a salesperson should always send an email confirming what the focus of the meeting is going to be. However, up to 50% of the salespeople we work with fail to set meeting expectations clearly. An example of such an expectation setting email is below.

Hi George,

Just a quick note to confirm our meeting at your office on Friday 24th March at 2pm.

As discussed I am looking forward to meeting with you to share some of our insights from CRM Systems implementations with companies such as; Megatek, Primo and Just Systems. In particular the key factors that determined the success of the implementations and some surprises along the way.

If there is anything else that you would like to cover or anybody else attending the meeting please let me know.

See you on Friday.

Regards

Paul

Remember, setting meeting expectations is an effective means of taking the pressure off both buyer and seller.

Sell With Stories

To engage with buyers the salesperson has to become a storyteller. Customer success stories are the most effective form of selling in initial customer encounters.

Stories 'pack a punch' far in excess of anything possible in respect of product data, elevator pitches or slide presentations. They are easier for people to listen to and engage with.

Stories are more vivid and easier to remember. In addition, they provide a greater element of authenticity, particularly when they reference other companies or individuals.

Furthermore, stories, by accessing the creative and imaginative side of the brain, enable the buyer to most effectively join the dots regarding their needs and the seller's solution.

Becoming A Storyteller

The transition from providing product and company information to sharing insights can pose challenges for many sales organizations. This is evidenced by the following questions that arise:

- What insights and stories are relevant to different customers or segments?
- Are they sufficiently topical and interesting to a potential customer?
- What if we don't know enough detail on the topic in question?
- How much expertise is required to deliver them credibly?
- What questions will they spark and can we answer them?
- What about issues of customer confidentiality?
- What if we cannot mention specifics or quantify results, for example?

Writing Customer Stories

Many sales teams are hampered by a lack of information regarding how their customers are using their solutions and the results being achieved.

We advise companies we work with to establish the following three processes to ensure they develop engaging and meaningful success stories that highlight their products and services.

1. **The project team:** For each significant project delivered a customer story must be developed by the account delivery team, under key headings such as:

   - The Customer
   - The Problem
   - The Solution
   - The Implementation/Process
   - The Results
   - The Surprises
   - The Quotes

2. **Internal project briefings:** Set-up internal project briefings where the sales team gets the opportunity to learn from those who have been directly involved in the project delivery.

3. **Engage a writer and marketing:** Engage a professional writer to compile the customer story, case study and whitepaper. Get marketing to ensure it becomes a key tool in the nurturing process.

6. EXPERT, NOT SALESPERSON

Buyers want to talk to experts, not salespeople. So the key to success for the salesperson is to make sure the buyer believes they have expert knowledge and access to expertise that is worth keeping in contact for.

Product Knowledge Is Never Enough

The number one complaint of buyers used to be lack of product knowledge on the part of the salesperson. But product knowledge is only part of the expertise equation. And product knowledge is no longer the primary interest of today's buyers. Buyers want to know how an offering will help their business meet its particular performance needs and challenges. Being able to show how this is achievable and adopting an advisory role is the mark of a true expert.

Become An Expert

Many salespeople have been re-packaged as consultants, advisors or specialists. But titles alone don't change the salesperson's level of product and industry knowledge, and credibility in the eyes of the buyer. They have to prove they have the ability to 'get down and dirty' when it comes to solving a customer's problems.

We asked a group of 65 professional B2B sales people in London if they considered themselves to be experts in their fields. Only five answered 'yes'.

Making the transition from 'salesperson' to 'expert' does present challenges. While it is just a small change in words, it requires a major change in attitude, skills levels and sales approach.

Being an expert not only requires a broad understanding of your products and services, but also of your client's business and industry.

As salespeople we must keep reminding ourselves:

- **The buyer has lots of ways of getting the information** regarding your solutions and those of your competitors. In fact, using information provided by analysts and the web is often seen as more objective.
- **Our products or services are not really what the customer needs**. They are simply a means of solving a problem or exploiting an opportunity. Our ability to discuss impact and results is what matters most. We must become experts in our solutions and how customers use and benefit from them. We need to constantly refresh our industry expertise.
- **The first step is to become an expert in your solutions** and how customers use and benefit from them. Then you need to become an expert in your industry and your marketplace.

There is a psychological advantage attached to being seen as an expert. Salespeople begin to walk taller and also begin to act a little different. Buyers begin to act differently too, opening doors, engaging more, listening more and trusting more.

Can You Pass The Test?

As a salesperson you have to pass one critical test. In the hours after your first sales meeting with a prospective client, does the client think of you as:

a) A salesperson who tried to sell something to them, or

b) An expert who had very interesting information and insights to share?

The reason why most sales meetings don't progress as planned is that most buyers leave meetings thinking they have met just another salesperson rather than an expert.

The bottom line is the first meeting with a buyer is never a 'sales meeting'. In fact, take away the word 'sales' and such meetings would be lot more effective for both the buyer and seller. So, stop selling and open up a dialogue that can develop over the coming weeks.

Are You An Expert?

Assess the likelihood a prospective client will see you as an expert rather than just another salesperson by answering the following questions:

1. Does the customer see you as qualified to help and advise them or simply as somebody trying to sell something?

2. Do you know the customers' industry, its opportunities and challenges?

3. Have you taken the time to really understand their business and its strategies?

4. Can you tell the customer how others have benefited from your solutions and in detail how they are using them?

5. Do you have some insights or information otherwise not available to the buyer?

6. Have you had enough product and industry training?

7. Are you certified?

8. Have you read leading research papers or attended key seminars on the industry, domain, category or the technology in question?

9. How visible is your profile as an expert? Have you written something, joined a professional body or given a talk?

Passion And Enthusiasm

In a world of grey suits and business formality, the level of passion and enthusiasm exhibited by the salesperson during a sales meeting is a rare opportunity to stand out from the crowd.

We sit through hundreds of sales presentations every year and regardless of the skill of the salesperson, the strength of the proposition or the timeliness of the message, what makes the real difference is the level of enthusiasm and passion of the salesperson.

Enthusiasm can be contagious. But if it appears the salesperson is not interested then how can the buyer be? Even if the salesperson has spent hours in traffic to get to the meeting and there is pressure to meet this month's target or the weather is bad, the salesperson has to make a determined effort to be enthusiastic at every sales encounter.

The danger is that where enthusiasm is not evident the buyer may mistake its absence for a lack of conviction or confidence regarding what is being sold. The buyer will rightly think 'if the salesperson is not enthusiastic about working with us before the order is won, then what hope is there of ensuring his full commitment after the sale.'

7. MAKE IT EASY TO SAY 'NO'

Buyers don't say no often enough. Believe it or not, for salespeople that can be a real problem. All too often weeks can be wasted chasing 'ghost opportunities' when you would be far better off knowing if your solution is at present not suitable or your timing is wrong.

Worse of all, many buyers have realized saying no is not necessarily the most effective way to get rid of a salesperson. Instead they ask for more information or even request a proposal as a means of keeping the salesperson at bay.

Don't Put Your Head In The Sand

The golden rule for sellers over the years was 'don't give the customer a chance to say no'. The logic was that by listing benefits and features with persistence and charm all the negatives would simply evaporate and you will eventually get the sale. This is a classic example of the 'ostrich theory' of selling.

However, in more complex sales situations that last anywhere from 6 to 18 months, you will want to hear a 'no' as much as a 'yes.' Getting a no in week two is much better than getting it in week 22, after time has been wasted on multiple futile calls, presentations and perhaps even a proposal. Your sales time is precious so make it easy for the customer to tell you if you are wasting your time or at least going in the wrong direction.

Assessing Buyer Interest

Here are some tips on sounding out the buyer in order to help both sides determine if there is a value in talking further at this time.

1. **Avoid making assumptions.** Check what you are talking about is of real interest.

2. **Ask questions** that relate to the insights you have presented. For example:

   - Do you think the client's experience is of relevance?
   - Is this something that you would be interested in exploring further?
   - Based on the results delivered what areas are most relevant to your situation?
   - Your business is no doubt different. Can you see any complicating factors?
   - Is this is a priority?
   - Is the timing right?
   - What view will the board take of such an investment?
   - What other projects are likely to be competing for resources?
   - Is there a budget available?

3. **Ask if there is a reason why this issue has not been addressed before**. If it has been examined before, find out what prevented its resolution. Have these obstacles been removed?

4. **Ask the buyer what they would like to do next**. Then offer some alternative next steps. Ask if there is anybody else that needs to be involved?

5. **Don't be afraid to ask 'big boy' questions**. If the seller feels there is a real hurdle to doing business that must be addressed before going any further. You should never shy away from asking difficult questions, such as:

   - 'I know you have a long-standing relationship with another supplier. Maybe I am wrong on this, but would you not be better off sticking with that company given the history that is there?'

- 'With all that is going on at the moment, do you think that this is a sufficient priority for your business at this time?'

6. **Share the homework.** Confirm interest by offering to do something (e.g. send on some information) and asking the buyer to do something in turn (e.g. forward a copy of a document that was mentioned or the name of a colleague that might be interested). This allows you to ensure buyer interest remains intact post the meeting.

Caution: Buyers Are Weary Of Questions

There is a reason why buyers sit back and let salespeople do all the talking — it puts them in control. This is particularly the case because salespeople ask fewer questions when they are talking — questions that buyers may be slow to answer because of:

- Political or other sensitivities.
- Genuine information gaps.
- Issues of confidentiality or trust.
- Perceived relevance or appropriateness.
- Issues of competitive fairness ('if I tell you I will have to tell all the others competing').
- Fear of giving the salesperson ammunition or being sold to.
- Not wanting to prejudice the seller's response/solution.

Buyers are also particularly weary of questions designed to:

- Box them in.
- Prequalify them.
- Uncover vulnerabilities.
- Highlight problems or inadequacies.
- Identify or accentuate points of pain.
- Hastily pinpoint a solution.
- Create tension that could cause change and disruption.

Remember, the objective of the initial meeting is not to develop a thorough understanding of the buyer's business or their needs. It is to start a conversation and to determine if the buyer and seller should be talking. So, put aside the detailed fact-finding or diagnostic tools, and focus on the conversation in the initial meeting.

Treat early stage meetings as exploratory meetings, to learn, share insights, understand priorities and help determine if you can offer a solution. This will allow you assess the level of interest in further conversation.

8. MAKE TIME FOR PREPARATION

Two thirds of salespeople we have surveyed say they rush underprepared into early stage sales meeting and, what is worse, buyers tell us that they can sense who is prepared and who is not. The result is that salespeople are turning up for sales meetings every day without being ready. They are failing to take full advantage of the limited time they have with the buyer and thus increasing the risk, that like so many other sales meetings, they end up going nowhere.

Essential Pre-Meeting Preparation

To be prepared and maximize the chances of success follow these straightforward steps:

1. Confirm the meeting, including who is to attend.

2. Clarify expectations for the meeting (e.g. format and agenda).

3. Do your homework on the company and its industry.

4. Research the person(s) being met (e.g. role and background).

5. Prepare relevant customer stories and insights.

6. Prepare a list of questions to ask or information to gather.

7. Prepare answers to questions and objections you will be asked.

8. Pack sales aides (e.g. reference letters or financial statements).

9. Decide what you want the buyer to think, say and do after meeting.

10. Consider the next step for both parties.

Spend Time Up Front, Save Time Later

Typically, your competition will spend lots of time and resources on the final proposal and sales presentation, but less comparable time preparing to make a good first impression on the prospect. That means the salesperson that spends more time preparing for initial meetings, will:

- Reduce the amount of time spent selling to those who can't buy.
- Build rapport faster by demonstrating a real interest in the prospect and their business.
- Relate more readily to the buyer's business and industry.
- Demonstrate professionalism by having their homework done.
- Have something much more interesting to talk to the buyer about.
- Maximize the time available for the meeting by ensuring they do not have to spend time asking for information that is readily available (for example, from the buyer's website).
- Avoid selling too early in the process.
- Have considered the next step that is most appropriate.
- Reduce any stress, allowing the buyer to feel more confident and comfortable during the meeting.

Savvy sales managers often advise their salespeople to do fewer, but better meetings. This is because there is always a trade-off to be made between quantity and quality of meetings.

Prequalify Before You Go

Leaving all the prequalification until the sales meeting often results in meetings that should not have gone ahead in the first place. So, in advance of the meeting and, indeed, before the meeting is arranged, the seller should ask themselves the following questions:

- Does the prospect fit the profile of a target customer for our business?
- Do we have something interesting to talk to them about?
- Can we bring some particular value to their business?
- Is there a problem in the public domain that they may have that we can solve?
- What problem/situation would need to exist for our service to be interesting to them?
- What evidence would suggest such a problem might exist?
- Why would such a problem not have been addressed to date?
- Are we talking to the right level in terms of functional responsibility and seniority?
- Should we continue to talk at this time?

Prepare To Be Quizzed

An essential means of preparing for sales meetings is to anticipate those questions that are likely to be asked and ensure that the answers are at the ready.

Thankfully, there is remarkable consistency in terms of the questions that buyers are likely to ask. With this in mind here are the top 15 questions compiled from a wide sample of meetings we have reviewed.

(a) When The Customer Is Exploring Alternatives

1. Why should we choose your company?

2. What are the advantages of your solution over others?

3. Why is your solution better than your competitors?

4. Why should we do this now, as opposed to next year? Why should we not find the solution in-house?

(b) When The Customer Is Looking For Confidence

5. Has the solution been bought by others in our industry?

6. Do you have an office in our region?

7. How strong is the financial backing of your company?

8. Has the solution been tested, verified or certified by any independent organization?

9. Can this prototype be piloted?

(c) The Cost-Benefit Equation

10. Our business is different. So, how can this work in our business?

11. I question your figures. Can that really be achieved?

12. Can the benefits be substantiated?

13. What is the return on investment?

14. What is the true cost? There must be other costs that need to be taken into consideration?

15. Why is it so expensive? What is the total cost of ownership? What is the payback on the investment?

Some of these 'killer' questions have the potential to stop the unprepared salesperson in their tracks. Preparing the answers won't just help you to impress the customer, it will also increase your level of comfort, credibility and effectiveness during the sales process.

Sticky Questions

We have learned over the years that most salespeople have at least one question that they fear being asked. That is a question or objection that strikes at the soft underbelly of their proposition — an area of potential vulnerability or weakness. In the case of a newer company, for example, it could be about their financial strength or track record. It is a question that, when it arises, is difficult to convincingly answer — something that the buyer is very quick to pick up on. What is your sticky question and have you found the best way to address it?

Preparing To Make A Great Impression

You never get a second chance to make a first impression. Therefore your personal presentation is everything. Your clothes and personal grooming shape how others see you, as well as how you feel about yourself. Salespeople need to maintain a very high standard of dress and grooming.

In fact, one client of ours took this issue so seriously that he put a giant mirror at the top of the stairs to underline the fact he expected the company's sales force to be well groomed at all times.

9. FOLLOW UP AND KEEP-IN-TOUCH

The initial meeting will hopefully be the start of a mutually beneficial relationship.

But a great first meeting is only as good as the degree of follow-up and follow-through.

Adopt A Multiple Meeting Mindset

Relationships cannot be built in one meeting. The first meeting is merely one step in the process of demonstrating your interest, credibility and trustworthiness. Even multi-million dollar investments all begin with a conversation, but when it comes down to it, not a lot can be achieved in the initial 40-minute sales meeting, apart from answering two fundamental questions:

Should we be talking?

Is this worth exploring at this time?

Remember, the one-meeting prequalification is an illusion. Getting the buyer to open up can take several meetings. Their true needs may not be immediately transparent, even to them, it's the salesperson's job to explore and develop them with the buyer. It can take time and several meetings for a salesperson to earn the right to ask many of the prequalification type of questions they are eager to have answered.

Adopt A Keep In-Touch Mindset

What do you do if the prospect is not ready, willing or able to buy? Most salespeople, although disappointed, pick themselves up and move on enthusiastically to the next sales meeting. Maybe that will be the one that uncovers a real and immediate sales opportunity.

Just because the company is not ready to buy from you today does not mean that they will never be in a position to buy. This is a point that was made with respect to lead generation and it is equally valid in respect of sales meetings. Situations change, new business needs emerge, managers come and go, priorities change and so do budgets. But are you going to be around when this happens? Are you going to be there when 'the light goes on' and suddenly the customer is in the market for a solution?

Keep The Conversation Going

If you believe you have the right solution you need absolute determination to keep the conversation going. On a prospect-by-prospect basis you must be determined and always keep in touch. If you do not, you leave the door open for another solution provider to come in and benefit from all your hard work. This requires you to take a long-term view.

Would you continue selling and developing relationships in an account for over three years without a result? Would you walk away? Say, you lost the deal to a competitor, would you shun the lost prospect and move on? Most salespeople would probably walk away. But one highly successful company we worked with did not. They took the rejection on the chin and kept in contact, making the calls and maintaining the relationship.

Yes, privately they complained of competitors playing dirty, but continued to make it easy for the customer to interact with their global teams. Finally, when there was a change of operations director in the account, the company secured a lucrative and strategic piece of business. It took a long time, but it did pay-off.

The 'Nobody Gets Left Behind' Mindset

High performing salespeople keep in touch with the entirety of their contact base. The level and frequency of this contact reflects the potential associated with each company in their database. They adopt a 'nobody gets left behind' philosophy. For example:

They diary a periodic telephone call, be that every six weeks or three months, to stay top of mind with those offering future potential. They also send an occasional email newsletter, article or information piece to those that represent 'long shots'.

However, good intentions are not enough. A CRM system (designed by the sales team for the sales team) is required to schedule periodic ongoing contact, making it easy to administer and ensuring it does not rely on the vagrancies of memory.

To avoid follow-on contact falling into the nuisance category, ensure the communication has a real value. For example, an article or whitepaper, a note regarding a move by one of their competitors or a link to a website containing useful information.

Mistakes to Avoid

Buyers are more demanding and less forgiving than ever before. This gives salespeople little margin for error. Below is a list of the most common, yet easily avoided, mistakes made by salespeople.

- **Suggesting we need your solution** without taking the time to find out about our needs or requirements. It is risky to assume the customer has a problem and needs your solution — so don't forget to ask first.
- **Claiming that your solution** meets every company's needs and failing to appreciate that our business is different or that our challenges are special.

- **Talking as if your solution is the only option**, making us suspect that you want to sell to us regardless.
- **Hinting that we do not know what we are doing** or that what we are doing is wrong. Surprisingly this is quite common, with many sales pitches beginning with a statement such as '80% of projects are over budget', 'most inventories are out by as much as 20%', etc. These can be viewed as thinly veiled insults to the customer.
- **Oversimplifying our requirements**. For example, suggesting easy integration with third-party systems, when we know that integration is never easy.
- **Making exaggerated claims** that detract from the credibility of their message. For example, 'reduces time to market from months to just hours', 'cuts integration costs by up to 90%', or 'can be implemented for just 10% of the cost of traditional solutions'. Your claims must be believable and backed-up by valid customer references.
- **Talking in terms of marketing fluff**, as opposed to objectively verifiable and quantifiable information. Also using confusing jargon of a technological nature.
- **Getting defensive when we ask questions** about your solution or not attaching enough importance to objections and questions raised.

The Sales Meeting Revolution — Summary

If sales teams are to succeed where they are currently failing, they need to embrace the new rules of sales meetings:

1. **Revise Your Objectives.** Sellers need to adjust their beliefs. Remember, just because a buyer has agreed to meet does not mean they want to be sold to. Treat early stage meetings as exploratory meetings, to learn, share insights, understand, help determine if you can offer a solution and assess the level of interest. Put the buyer's agenda ahead of your own.

2. **Slow Down, Stop Selling.** Sales teams are selling too fast and too soon. Even though salespeople are under increased pressure to sell, the introductory meetings are definitely not the place to do it. Sellers must resist the temptation to propose solutions and deliver presentations.

3. **Hold Conversations, Not Presentations.** Most sales pitches and presentations are based on delivering a monologue as opposed to building a dialogue between buyer and seller. The most effective sales meetings are not actually sales meetings at all, they are conversations. Start the conversation and build the dialogue.

4. **Listen, Before Talking.** Contrary to popular opinion great sales people are not great talkers, but great communicators. The key difference is the ability to listen. Start the conversation and engage the buyer, listen and learn their perspective. Remember it is not about you, it is about them.

5. **Share Insights, Not Information.** Communicate compelling stories of how customers have benefited and how industries are changing, and forget the features and benefits for now. Buyers want something more than marketing blurb and techno babble in return for the time they invest in a meeting. Sellers need to brush up on their ability to tell executive stories.

6. **Think Expert, Not Salesperson.** Buyers want to know how an offering will help their business meet its particular performance needs and challenges. Products or services are not really what the customer needs. They are simply a means of solving a problem or exploiting an opportunity. The seller's ability to talk impact and results is what matters most. They must become experts in their solutions and how customers use and benefit from them. Sellers need to constantly refresh their industry expertise.

7. **Make It Easy To Say 'No'.** Sellers need to help buyers to say 'no' and thereby prevent either party wasting time. 'No', 'not now', or 'not quite' can tell the salesperon if and when he, or she should invest time in a prospect.

8. **Make Time for Preparation.** The seller that spends more time preparing for initial meetings will have a real advantage.

9. **Keep In Touch.** Just because the company is not ready to buy from you today does not mean that they will never be in a position to buy. Situations change, new business needs emerge, managers come and go, priorities change and so do budgets. Are you going to be around when this happens?

These steps will help increase the effectiveness of early stage meetings and prompt open dialogue based on the opportunity to deliver bottom line impact to the buyer. Inevitably more in-depth discussions and workshops will be required. Now, at this critical stage, the seller needs to ensure their sales cycle is mapped to the buyer's buying process.

SECTION 9:

The Sales Cycles Revolution

THE NEW RULES FOR SALES OPPORTUNITIES

Salespeople are under more pressure than ever to sell. But more selling is not the answer. That is because, generally speaking, it does not help buyers to buy. So, what exactly is required to progress buyers who show an interest?

Sellers have come to realize that what happens from the point of the first meeting to just before the proposal is submitted has a major impact on the likelihood of a sale. This is what we call the effective management of sales cycles or opportunities and it offers the greatest potential to boost sales success.

This chapter will challenge your beliefs about the role of the sales process, how to accelerate the sale and the way buyers look at needs and solutions. It will demonstrate how sellers can help buyers to navigate their internal buying processes and move in the direction of the buying decision.

More Selling Is Not The Answer

Sales professionals at all levels must realize the new basis for competition is not selling, but buying. Those **sales organizations who really understand how buying has changed and who successfully adapt how they sell to reflect these changes, will outsell their competition.**

The role of the salesperson is to help the buyer to buy. For professional sellers this is a major shift in mindset. However, this shift will prevent a mad dash for the order, the futile preparation of 'hit and miss' sales proposals and misguided attempts to accelerate the sale.

Adopting the Buying Perspective

To improve win rates salespeople need to embrace the *Seven New Rules* in respect of how sales cycles are managed:

1. Think Buying Process, Not Sales Process.
2. Think Business Decision, Not Buying Decision.
3. To Speed Up, Slow Down.
4. Access is a Privilege, Not a Right.
5. First Needs, Then Solutions.
6. Think Total Solution.
7. Review Early and Often.

1. THINK BUYING PROCESS, NOT SALES PROCESS

To turn the complexity of modern buying in your favor it is vital to focus on the process the buyer must follow, as opposed to idealized notions of the sale. However, of the hundreds of salespeople we surveyed, 90% are using the same sales tools and techniques for more than a decade.

As a result, selling today is at odds with how organizations buy. In many cases the gap between buying and selling is widening, because the traditional sales process obstructs a clear view of modern buying decisions.

Why Your Sales Process Won't Save You

Longer and more complex buying decisions mean it is more difficult to predict what deals will close and when. To tackle this uncertainty, sales managers have stepped up the search for a more consistent and repeatable process for converting leads to orders.

However, many managers are wasting their time tweaking sales processes that are at odds with how buyers buy. Because of the increased sophistication of modern buying the priority must be to transform, rather than just systemize, how organizations sell.

Ensure Your Process Is the Right Process

Every seller needs a defined sales process that can be consistently applied in the marketplace. To ensure your organization's process is the right process it must avoid the following dangers:

1. **The sales process often seeks to dictate how buyers should buy.** However, the reality is that buying process trumps sales process every time. Buyers have their own internal processes to follow — processes that are increasingly demanding. The seller's sales process does not carry any weight with the senior management who determine project approval.

2. **The sales process often over-simplifies buying.** The result is sales methods that are out of sync with the changing information requirements of buyers, the numbers involved in the buying decision or the various stages of the buying process. If the wrong sales processes are standardized then that will only deliver the wrong results more consistently with poor conversion rates being accepted as the norm.

3. **The sales process creates a dangerous illusion of control** on the part of the seller. Increasingly buyers are rebelling against the 'self-serving' sales processes of vendors. They will stubbornly refuse to be corralled through the seller's sales funnel. All salespeople need to understand the buyer is in control, not the seller.

4. The sales process often entails **the systematic application of techniques that are increasingly rejected by buyers**. After all, if buyers don't want to be sold to then why do managers think that selling to them in a more consistent and repeatable manner is the answer? The reality is there are parts of most sales processes that buyers would find objectionable. They must be removed.

5. **The sales process does not help buyers to buy.** It often reflects a view of selling as something that is done to, as opposed to with, buyers. It tends to be focused on getting the sale, as opposed to helping the buyer to make the right business decision. Putting the buyer first means focusing on the buying process not the sales process.

6. **The sales process tends to make assumptions** about how buyers will buy. Assumptions that can be dangerous. Salespeople need to understand the various procedures behind how each buying decision is made.

7. **The sales process seeks consistency**, yet buyers are increasingly divergent in terms of how they buy. The rigid application of the sales process mistakenly treats all buyers as if they are the same. Sellers must be flexible in responding to the specific decision-making requirements of each buying situation. The salesperson cannot be slave to two masters — it is the buyer and their process that must have the final say.

8. Sales processes by their very nature tend to be **focused on the seller and self-serving**. In addition there are often aspects of sales process that buyers consider to be manipulative. So, if you cannot lay out your sales process in front of a buyer without the risk of offending them then its time to revisit it. Your process, if it's the right one, should help the buyer navigate their buying process and make the decision easier.

A Rethink Is Needed

It is time for sales processes, sales methodologies and sales techniques to take a back seat to the way of the buyer. For the sales organization that means the sales process must be overhauled to reflect the full complexity of modern buying and ensure flexibility in responding to the unique buying requirements of each potential customer.

When we sampled 120 companies that sell complex solutions, only 5% had a clearly defined sales process outlining the best way to sell to their customers. Their approach varies from sale to sale and from salesperson to salesperson. Even fewer had adapted their sales process to the changed nature of organizational buying.

> **BUYER INSIGHT**
>
> 'The seller's sales process should enrich the buyer. It should help to facilitate the steps we are required to follow to make a decision.'
>
> Operations Director, Global Telecoms Company

Think Buying Process _Not_ Sales Process

Does your organization put its sales process ahead of the client's buying process? Take the test overleaf.

Q1. What is most important when it comes to selling?
(a)   Your sales process ☐ (b) The buyer's process   ☐

Q2. How consistently is your sales process applied?
(a)   Rigidly   ☐ (b) Flexibly   ☐

Q3. How would you describe your buyer's procurement process?
(a)   Unsophisticated ☐ (b) Sophisticated   ☐

Q4. Do you believe you know more than the buyer?
(a)   Yes   ☐ (b) No   ☐

Q5. How would you describe the role of the salesperson?
(a)   To sell, sell, sell! ☐ (b) To help buyers buy   ☐

Q6. What is your level of understanding of your customers buying process?
(a)   Patchy   ☐ (b) Thorough   ☐

Q7. How would you describe your sales process?
(a)   Unilateral   ☐ (b) Consultative   ☐

Q8. Has your sales process changed over the last three years?
(a)   No   ☐ (b) Yes   ☐

Q9. Who do you believe should be in control?
(a)   The Salesperson ☐ (b) The Buyer   ☐

Q10. How important are the latest sales techniques?
(a)   Important   ☐ (b) Not Important   ☐

How did you score? If you answered (a) to between two and four of the questions you are at risk of developing an obsession with the sales process, instead of buying process. If you answered (a) to five or more then your obsession with sales process is total and the buying process is your organization's blind spot.

Making The Buying Process Your Ally

An increasing number of sales professionals recognize that by focusing on the buying process they can turn the complexity of modern buying to their advantage. Here are nine steps organizations we work with follow to make the buying process central to sales success:

1. KNOW The Buying Process
2. RESPECT The Buying Process
3. ADAPT To The Buying Process
4. START Earlier In The Buying Process
5. INVEST More In The Buying Process
6. FACILITATE The Buying Process
7. BECOME A Trusted Advisor In The Buying Process
8. ENSURE Integrity In The Buying Process
9. DEFER To The UMPIRE Of The Buying Decision

Now let us examine each of these steps in more detail.

1. KNOW The Buying Process

From the countless number of pipeline reviews we participate in, it is clear that there is a lack of understanding of what must happen on the buyer side before a purchasing decision can be made.

Too often salespeople are making dangerous assumptions. This is simply because they fail to ask the buyer about how the decision will be made and how they can assist in that process. The seller must put themselves in the buyer's shoes to really appreciate the more subtle aspects of the buying decision — the politics, the reporting relationships, the culture, the history, the risks and concerns.

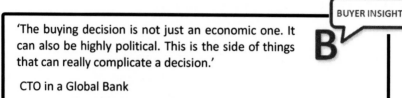

'The buying decision is not just an economic one. It can also be highly political. This is the side of things that can really complicate a decision.'

CTO in a Global Bank

2. RESPECT The Buying Process

Sellers must respect the buying process and obey its rules. Rather than trying to circumvent it, they must adhere to every step and facilitate the buyer in meeting all its requirements. In particular, sellers must not attempt to close the sale before key aspects of the buying process have been completed and agreed.

Sellers must never undermine the buyer. It is vital they always get permission from the buyer before making contact with any of the other stakeholders or decision-makers involved in the buying process. *'The one certain way to get the buyer's back up and consequently get yourself disqualified, is to go around the buyer and talk to others without his agreement,'* a senior executive in a telecoms company informed us.

It is also important to respect the wisdom of the buyer and the buying process. Today's buyer may well know as much if not more than the salesperson. They also have access to domain experts and specialist advisors to the buying decision. The seller should focus on supporting and facilitating, as opposed to second-guessing, the buyer.

3. ADAPT To The Buying Process

Don't try to impose your own process on the buyer. Although this sounds obvious, buyers tell us that it happens quite regularly. In most cases, however, it is not a conscious decision on the part of the salesperson to try to direct the buyer in a particular way, but rather a failure to elicit from the buyer how they may want to proceed. Even though the buyer may appear to be acquiescing to the seller's process, the buyer's process will always take precedence.

The salesperson must actively reflect the way the buyer is going to buy right from what is discussed at the first meeting to the terminology, metrics and format of the final proposal.

> **BUYER INSIGHT**
>
> **B**
>
> Three vendors were shortlisted to bid for an IT systems sale valued at approximately €3 million. Each received a telephone call asking to kick off the process with a presentation to the buying team.
>
> 'We would like to do a technical audit first and to receive at least an outline specification of requirements,' replied the sales manager of the number one contender and global leader.
>
> 'Does that mean you are not interested in presenting?' asked the CTO in the buying organization. The manager did not directly say no, but the lack of enthusiasm put the buyer off. A more compliant alternative vendor was selected to present and tender instead.

4. START Earlier In The Buying Process

The highly structured nature of the buying process requires the salesperson to get involved earlier. That is before the budget is allocated, before the requirements are set and perhaps even before the buying has started.

Salespeople are being called upon later in the sales cycle and then arriving into a competitive bidding situation. When this happens the salesperson may at best have a 50:50 chance of success. However, the salesperson that gets involved earlier by nurturing the relationship and shaping the need, will always be in pole position once the buying decision reaches an advanced stage.

5. INVEST More In The Buying Process

The new complexity of buying decisions requires more from salespeople. More information is required, more people are involved and more interaction is needed if the sale is going to progress smoothly. For example, most salespeople we work with have contact with no more than two or three people in their target accounts. However, according to buyers, the numbers involved in shaping the buying decision in most large organizations typically ranges from six to eight.

While lengthening sales cycles put sellers under increased pressure and significantly impacts on the cost of sale, there is no option but to invest more time and effort in each buying process.

6. FACILITATE The Buying Process

Stop selling and help the buyer make the best decision for their business. Your job is to facilitate that decision and provide the information that helps the buyer to more clearly define their requirements.

7. BECOME A Trusted Advisor In The Buying Process

Buyers are increasingly cautious of who they will take advice from. In particular they have learned to be wary of traditional salespeople and their approaches. So, to become an active participant in shaping the buying decision is a real privilege.

Only salespeople who can display the characteristics of a trusted advisor will win a seat at the buying table. Of course, expertise is vitally important. The buyer has to recognize the salesperson has valuable knowledge and expertise to add. Moreover, the salesperson has to demonstrate a genuine commitment to helping the buyer.

8. ENSURE Integrity In The Buying Process

Most salespeople have discovered a long time ago that a genuine interest in helping the buyer goes a long way to success. As a result they shun crude and manipulative sales techniques such as:

- Mirroring and pacing buyer behavior.
- Closing techniques, from the 'half Nelson' to 'standing room only'.
- Flimsy conditioning techniques.
- False flattery or insincerity.
- 'Good cop, bad cop' and other negotiation stances.

When dealing with sophisticated buyers, integrity and intent are more important than technique. In this respect a genuine interest in helping the buyer and their business succeed is what matters most.

9. DEFER To The UMPIRE Of The Buying Decision

There is an umpire involved in most major purchasing decisions — the purchasing department. Indeed, recognition of the strategic role of purchasing is a key reason why buying has become a lot more sophisticated (something that was discussed in Part 1). Purchasing has to be involved if a decision is going to be sanctioned. So, if purchasing is not at the table after three meetings, the salesperson must ask if they should be talking to them.

Do You Fully Understand The Buying Process?

Take the top three opportunities in your sales pipeline and explore how well you understand the buying process in each situation by answering the following questions:

1. Who are all the stakeholders?

2. Who are all the decision makers and influencers?

3. Is there a clear definition of the requirements?

4. What is the buying process? How sophisticated is it?

5. What are the key steps?

6. How advanced is the buying process at this time?

7. How long will it take?

8. What documentation is required as part of the process?

8. Are there competing projects (that includes the 'do it in-house' option)?

8. Is a business case required? If yes:

      - What format will it take?

      - Who is responsible for its production?

9. What is the role of procurement?

10. Is there a shortlist of vendors? How many? What is the criterion?

11. At what level is final sign-off required?

12. Who is in the role of business analyst (the person acting as the bridge between technical and business)?

This is a shortened list of those questions presented at the close of Sections 2, 3 and 4 of Part 1, The Buying Revolution™.

SELLER INSIGHT

A salesperson diligently created a list of 80 companies ideally suited to buying her company's solutions. After making initial contact with the companies, the salesperson managed to organize a handful of meetings and finally established three real prospects — a response rate of 5%.

For several quarters the salesperson progressively nurtured the list, sending occasional whitepapers, detailed customer success stories, and followed up with a keep-in-touch phone call. Over time changes in personnel and in priorities resulted in a steady trickle of additional sales meetings, cycles and orders. The salesperson had ensured she was there 'when the light went on' and the need became a priority. Ultimately that resulted in a hit rate three-times the original response rate from the list.

2. BUSINESS DECISIONS, NOT BUYING DECISIONS

Sellers can radically increase their success by looking beyond the purchase order to the business decision upon which it depends. By not looking beyond the buying decision, the seller fails to see that the real competition is not from another supplier, but from other competing projects or priorities in the buying organization. The result is that the salesperson is busy trying to convince the buyer to buy, when they should be helping the buyer build a compelling business case.

Why Buying Decisions Get Stalled

Buying decisions don't get stalled because the buyer cannot chose between one supplier and another. Rather, because a compelling business rationale for the purchase has not been established. So the lesson for salespeople is to look after the business decision and the buying decision will inevitably follow.

The Business Behind Buying

So, what is the key difference between the business decision and the buying decision? Well, the business decision is more concerned with the 'why' or business rationale of the decision, while the buying decision is often more concerned with the 'how'. The business decision is focused on the impact of the purchase on the performance, objectives and strategy of the business.

Most buying decisions cannot be made unless the underlying business rationale has been clearly demonstrated. So, behind every major purchasing decision, and many smaller ones too, is an important business decision. It is much more complex than any issues surrounding product features or supplier capability. The question is — does how you sell take this into account?

> **BUYER INSIGHT**
>
> After countless customer visits, sales presentations and a sales proposal, the salesperson was getting impatient. He had been told they were the forerunner of the three possible suppliers being considered. But what was taking the buyer so long to decide? The cycle had entered its ninth month and it was the end of the quarter. After an internal review of the account with his CEO, a decision was taken to call the CTO of the buying organization.
>
> After a few pleasantries, the CEO cut to the chase asking 'How is the selection process progressing?' The CTO replied that 'there was a lot going on in the company and it would be at least the next quarter before the situation would become clear.'
>
> As the CEO hung up the phone he was no closer to the sale than his salesperson before him. The CTO did not tell him the real reason things had slowed down — they had not established a compelling business case and the buyer's CFO needed to be involved in the process.

Selling To The Business Decision

To find out if a sales opportunity hinges on a straight-forward buying decision or a more complex business decision you need to answer the following questions:

- How important is the purchase to the business?
- How will it impact on the business and its performance?
- What are the key business drivers and constraints impacting on a decision?
- How does it fit with past decisions, as well as present goals and strategies?
- What key business performance metrics will be used to measure success?
- What other projects are competing for the same resources?

- What level of planning and analysis must underpin the decision?
- At what level of senior management within the organization will the purchase decision be made or reviewed?

Focusing On The Business Decision

Buyers will not buy unless it makes clear business sense. That means helping a buyer to establish the business rationale behind the purchase is the job of the sales team. This however requires a focus beyond the purchase order.

Focusing on the business decision results in a major overhaul of traditional features and benefits selling. It is fundamental to boosting sales success. But there are other advantages too. Understanding and influencing the business dimension makes for more realistic pipeline forecasts and better opportunity management. It also represents a key step in the evolution from salesperson to trusted advisor.

The salesperson that helps shape the business decision has reached the pinnacle of selling. They have influence and power way beyond that of the majority of salespeople who are merely chasing the purchase order.

Such high-level sales professionals are characterized by the following six behaviors. They:

- Talk Results.
- Talk To Decision Makers.
- Talk To Non-Technical Buyers.
- Ask Better Questions.
- Connect With Goals and Strategies.
- Face The Real Competition.

Let us examine each of these in turn.

1. Talk Results

The salesperson focused on facilitating the business decision is having much more interesting conversations, by:

- Talking about results before talking about features and benefits.
- Packing sales materials and presentations with details of results achieved by other customers.
- Quantifying results using the key metrics of interest to the buyer (e.g. cost per transaction, cost per data access point, cost per health and safety breach).
- Helping the buyer model the results to highlight what can be achieved in their business.

It is worth noting that talking results may require a crash course in accounting principles (but we will look at this issue in more detail later).

2. Talk To Decision Makers

The salesperson focused on the business decision is talking to more interesting people. That is to those who have the authority to make business decisions, to change priorities and to allocate budgets. They are increasingly talking to C-level managers — to the CTO, the CFO or the board.

As we will see later this can present challenges. Such high-level executives are not easy to access or engage. They also require different topics of conversation, as they won't be interested in monologues based on features and benefits.

3. Talk To Non-Technical Buyers

In focusing on the business decision, the salesperson talks with financial and business stakeholders, not just with the technical buyer. That means spending more time with the right people.

The salesperson must seek out the business analyst acting as the bridge between technical or operational aspects of the purchase and the business case. If such a role does not exist it is particularly important the salesperson helps to compensate for its absence. That means ensuring both business and technical sides of the buying organization are reconciled around a common business case and solution.

4. Ask Better Questions

The salesperson working the business decision is asking buyers better questions — that is those shown on the right-hand-side of the table below. These are the questions that uncover real needs and most powerfully match them to the seller's solutions.

BUYING DECISION QUESTIONS	BUSINESS DECISION QUESTIONS
• What is the criterion for ideal solution? • What is the criterion for best supplier? • What is the budget? • Where is the budget coming out of? • What is the desired feature set? • What are the specifications? • How long before a decision is made? • What are the best terms? • What is 'the best deal'? • How will it be delivered? • Who will sign the order? • What paperwork is required?	• What is the business case? • What are the objectives? • How does it fit with our strategy? • How will it improve performance? • What are all the options and alternatives? • What is the expected payback? • What is the total cost of ownership? • What are the risks? • What people & process issues exist? • How will we ensure implementation success? • What are your peers in other companies doing? • Have the stakeholders agreed? • Will senior managers sign it off? • Are there competing projects?

5. Connect With Goals And Strategies

An ability to see the business dimension of the buying decision requires an understanding of the buyer's business and industry. It also requires connecting with the goals and strategies of the buying organization.

In particular, it draws attention to the top priorities, including the present drive to cut costs, drive efficiency and minimizing risk. It also brings into focus the business drivers and constraints that impact on the sale, including people, politics, culture and strategic fit.

6. Face The Real Competition

Those that focus on the buying decision realize the main competition today is often not another vendor, but another project or course of action within the buying organization. With scarce organizational resources, businesses must make choices between projects, priorities and strategies that are competing for the same resources.

The job of the salesperson is to help to make the project more compelling than its alternatives, including a decision to do the work in-house, to choose an alternative technology or the most common decision of all — to delay making a decision.

3. TO SPEED UP, SLOW DOWN

Sales managers dream of shorter sales cycles, but the reality is that to speed up the sale they may need to slow down their selling.

Longer sales cycles have serious implications for meeting sales targets and controlling sales costs, as well as for the overall level of sales visibility, predictability and control. However, a slower sale is better than a lost sale due to impatience.

Speed Is Not Everything

Accelerating key aspects of the sale is a mistake. Indeed, salespeople must slow down certain key steps if they are to be effective.

Even though the salesperson may have seen the situation hundreds of times before and can clearly see the problem, it is important they slow down in order to understand all the nuances, including the political and organizational context.

Sellers also need to take time before asking too many questions, particularly invasive ones. Remember, the salesperson has to earn the right to ask questions.

Salespeople need to slow down before proposing a solution. It is vital they take time to understand the buyer's full range of needs, jointly explore solutions and build rapport in the process.

It is also important the salesperson takes their time before writing a proposal. The faster a proposal is written the more assumptions it is likely to contain and the less likely it is to involve the buyer in its creation.

A sales cycle that is progressing slowly needs more interaction not less, it requires more time not less and it may even mean retracing some of the steps that have already been taken. Indeed, if a decision is stalled it may mean that you should go right back to square one. Understanding the buying decision, reappraising needs and exploring solution alternatives is the only option.

> **SELLER INSIGHT**
>
> A veteran sales manager who has sold more than a half of a billion in IT systems over the past decade was often heard saying, 'If there is a change in personnel in a buying unit you have to go back to square one'. Frustrating and annoying — yes! But essential!

Walk, Don't Run

You cannot run through a complex buying cycle. You need to be precise and walk through it one step at a time or risk losing the buyer and potentially the sale. This can also require ensuring the buyer slows down too.

Take for example a potential client who is in a rush to get a proposal after just two or three meetings. It can be tempting for the salesperson to jump at the opportunity, but doing so may jeopardize the sale.

A proposal written without sufficient interaction is a real shot in the dark and something that is likely to do more harm than good. After all, how can you expect to fully understand the needs of stakeholders, define a solution (that will deliver high impact and high value) and set a budget based on a few conversations lasting just 40 or so minutes?

While taking the time to gather key information may mean moving the opportunity out by a month or quarter, it is likely to dramatically increase the likelihood of success.

How You Sell Is How You Service

In the past the salesperson's job was to match the specifications to the requirements and close the deal. But in today's complex sales environment it requires a lot more, because establishing the requirements and defining the specification can be a major part of the solution in itself. That means the solution and how it is sold are inseparable.

The salesperson's job is not just to sell, but to add value through the sales process. They are required to bring the service into the selling, creating the solution as part of the sales process and perhaps even delivering elements of it before the final buying decision is made (e.g. scoping projects, proof of concepts, consulting projects and pilots).

The fact is buyers give due consideration to how an organization sells. They use it as an important barometer to judge the service level they can expect once they complete their selection process. The level of expertise and professionalism experienced by prospects has a direct impact on win rates.

Take Care To Accelerate The Right Process

The only possible way to accelerate the sale is to accelerate the business and buying decisions that underpin it. However, as the complex buying processes examined in Part 1 demonstrates, buyers cannot race to the purchase order even if they want to.

Sellers cannot go from a sales meeting to a sales proposal and skip the vital step of interacting with the buyer and their needs. The seller that attempts to lure the buyer across the line purely with their credentials and value proposition will always struggle. Making the decision requires a compelling business rationale. That means sellers must invest more time helping the buyer establish the need for the solution and build a compelling business case (something we will discuss in the next section).

So, the only way to accelerate a sales process is to start it earlier and thereby to make it longer.

'Our sales cycles are long, there is no question about that, but it depends on when you start the clock. If you start it at the initial point of contact with our telemarketing then they are 12-16 months. If you start counting back from the first meeting with a salesperson then they are 8-10 months.

It seems obvious but the key to shorter sales cycles is to try to get involved with the potential customer at the earliest point in their buying process. Marketing is now running a "keep in touch" program that allows our salespeople to work with those that are at the right stage for what are active sales cycles. It's not just a sales effort, it's joined-up thinking with sales and marketing working hand-in-hand.'

Sales Manager, Electronics Manufacturer

4. ACCESS IS A PRIVILEGE, NOT A RIGHT

Even though there are six to eight decision makers involved in any buying decision, salespeople tend to only have access to half that number. Even more troubling is that these contacts tend to typically be those of lower rank within the buying organization.

No Access, No Sale

To win the sale the salesperson must first win access to the boardroom. This is where the real decision is going to be made. However, while access is the essential currency of the complex sale, it is in short supply.

Based our involvement in campaigns targeting thousands of managers in the UK and North America, we have seen executive access decline by 50% in five years. In other words, it takes twice as long to reach a C-level executive in a major organization than it did five years ago.

Little wonder then that salespeople are complaining about their ability to access the people and the information they need to win the sale. Without access and information sales presentations and proposals involve more guesswork than ever before. Such guesswork has an adverse affect on every sales team's closure rate.

SELLER INSIGHT

'We were disheartened by the loss of the latest deal, but struggled to understand what we had done wrong. We badly needed the work so lessons had to be learned.

We did a little soul searching asking questions, such as: "Who was the sponsor?", "How many people were involved in the buying group?", and "How much interaction did we really have with the seller?"

Suddenly, the problem became clear. We had only met with two people from the buying company and most of the interaction, besides a formal presentation, had taken place through the 'sponsor' who managed access to the buying team. More worrying still, the sponsor was an independent consultant whose role, influence and allegiance we did not fully understood at the time.

We set a new rule of thumb — before preparing a proposal for submission for future prospects we must talk to at least four people and have at a minimum four meetings.'

Director of Business Development, International Architectural Firm

Access Has To Be Earned

While you will obviously want to talk to all those in the buying team, as well as other key stakeholders, the question is — why would they want to talk to you?

Managers are busy people, and as a result they don't have much time to spend with salespeople. In many cases even if they had the time they would choose to spend it doing something else. They don't like being sold to. Thus access to senior managers is a privilege granted to only those that can bring value and insights to the table.

Sellers often complain of being kept at arm's length by buyers, but to get access salespeople need to earn it. Access will depend on the perceived level of professionalism, commitment, expertise, as well as the likeability or trustworthiness of the salesperson. Of course, it also depends on the perceived importance and reputation of the vendor they work for.

HOW TO LOSE ACCESS	HOW TO WIN ACCESS
• Talk too much about yourself. • Sound like a 'know-it-all.' • Don't listen or show empathy. • Ask inappropriate questions. • Evade questions, start bluffing. • Go over or around the buyer. • Use statements such as 'trust me!' • Bad mouth competitors. • Say you can do everything. • Use crude closing techniques. • Tell stories that suggest a breach of confidence. • Rush to provide a solution, before fully understanding needs. • Try to hurry or pressurize the buyer.	• Focus on helping, not selling. • Demonstrate professionalism and respect. • Follow the rules of engagement. • Provide useful information. • Share your expertise. • Don't try to impose your sales process. • Show a genuine interest in the buyer. • Earn the right to ask questions. • Understand requirements before advocating a solution. • Be passionate about your industry. • Explain why you need access. • Treat people's time as precious. • Use workshops to deliver outputs.

Those that do gain access are unlikely to be seen as salespeople at all, at least not in the traditional sense. Rather they are likely to be considered specialists, advisors, consultants or experts.

Reasons Why Access Is Not Granted

Here are some of the key barriers sellers hear when they ask for greater access, in particular to senior managers:

- 'They are busy and don't have time.'
- 'If you tell me the information you want I will get it for you.'
- 'If they were to talk to you then they would have to talk to all companies bidding.'
- 'To maintain fairness we must stick within the competitive bidding framework.'
- 'We don't want to prejudice the outcome or suggested solution'.
- 'It is too early — there will be an opportunity to present later on'.
- 'I will pass you on to IT, procurement or the consultants that are handling that'.

So, the salesperson must be able to overcome these objections, as well as the underlying antipathy towards salespeople generally. They must present a clear rationale for access and explain how it will benefit the buyer.

The Rules Of Access

Here are some guidelines that buyers have told us are important to gaining and maintaining access.

1. **Always obey the rules regarding access**, don't go over or around others to speak to the stakeholders that you want.
2. **Map the buying process to the organizational chart** to identify who you need to meet. Then pair it with your team as appropriate (e.g. CFO to your CFO).
3. **Tell them why you want to meet**, ask them what they want to get from it and set a clear agenda in advance.

4. **Take advantage of other means of interacting** with those managers of interest, for example, industry association events, conferences and sporting events.

5. **Use access sparingly** and plan it to get the most from any time you have with stakeholders. That includes meeting at the right time in the process to get most value from it. For example, before meeting the executive buying team, make sure you have your initial briefing or scoping completed with their direct reports.

6. **Do your homework in advance** and make sure you are fully prepared. Don't waste time gathering information in the meeting that you could have found from the company's website or annual report.

7. **Research the key participants** involved in the buying team to understand their role, their previous positions, their qualifications and any contacts you have in common.

8. **Consider the use of workshops** that have a value to the buyer as a means of making access efficient. For example, a workshop on defining requirements, completing the business case, trends and best practice.

9. **Watch the clock.** Make sure meetings and presentations don't go on for longer than they have to.

10. **Reward the buyer for their time.** Provide the buyer with useful insights and information to aid the decision-making process. Provide tools and templates that can support eliciting requirements, defining the specification, building the business case and making the business decision.

11. **Adopt a consultative approach.** Don't assume the buyer needs your help or that your metrics, models and analysis are what they want.

12. **Tailor the approach** to the functional background and seniority of the manager in question, in particular relating to their key priorities and metrics.

13. **Be judicious and tactful** regarding the questions you ask of the buyer, remember you have to earn the right to ask questions that are invasive or sensitive.

14. **Set a follow-up action and promptly send a** note with a summary of the meeting and some useful piece of follow-up material or information for the buyer.

15. **Keep your main contact in the loop** regarding any meetings you have with their colleagues.

No Access, No Way

Clearly, there is no point in salespeople doing all the running unless the buyer is at least following. If the buyer is not prepared to engage then the likelihood of a successful outcome is low and the opportunity may not be worth pursuing. Maybe they do not understand your value or the benefits of your solution or perhaps it is not sufficiently important to the buyer at this time. Just as buyers get to choose when and how to engage, so too can vendors. In particular there may be situations where a seller should decide to walk away. This is something that is examined in more detail in Section 5: Revolutionizing Orders, rule number 6: 'Walk if You Cannot Talk'.

The Engagement Barometer

If access can be difficult to win, engagement is even more challenging. Decision makers may be readily available, but without real engagement the salesperson is lost at sea.

Salespeople increasingly complain that buyers are playing their cards close to their chest. The result is that they 'are left to do all the running'. Far from selling being a joint-venture exercise, the buyer can easily be a passive participant. This poses a problem for the salesperson who wants to work with the buyer to explore alternatives and find the best solution.

Answer the following questions to explore the level of engagement buyers grant you:

1. Can you pick up the phone and meet the buyer whenever you need to?
2. Has there been any social contact with the buying team — has an interpersonal dimension to the relationship developed?
3. Does the buyer call you unsolicited looking for information or advice?
4. Have you been able to talk to all those involved in the buying decision?
5. Do you have all the information you need?
6. Have you got all the questions you need answered?
7. Have you been able to review internal documentation?
8. Have you been told how the buying decision is going to be made?
9. Is there a good working relationship?
10. Has the buyer completed all the items that were agreed?
11. Has there been good two-way interaction during meetings?
12. Is there good follow-up and follow-through by the buyer?
13. Is there a high level of openness?
14. Has the buyer taken you into their trust?
15. Can you raise any concerns or issues that arise?
16. Is there mutual respect, including for each other's time?
17. Is there ownership of the solution?
18. Has it been arrived at jointly?
19. Is there a two-way exchange of ideas?
20. Is there feedback on proposals and presentations?
21. Is documentation jointly prepared and reviewed?
22. Does the buyer value your opinion, seek your advice, ask you to help prepare documentation and enlist your help in navigating the buying process?
23. Do you have a sponsor on the buying team?
24. Have you been given the 'inside track' regarding the buying decision, including complicating factors, issues of politics and so on?

5. FIRST NEEDS, THEN SOLUTIONS

Salespeople spend nine-times longer talking about their solutions and companies than about the needs of the buyer. This means they are up to nine-times more likely to get it wrong.

How do you know if you are more focused on the buyer's needs rather than your solution? Review the language you use in sales pitches, presentations and proposals, and using the table below circle the words that dominate your sales vocabulary.

OLD: FOCUSED ON SELLER	NEW: FOCUSED ON BUYER
• Competitive Advantage	• Success
• Unique Selling Points	• Priorities
• Value Proposition	• Results/Impact
• Our Company	• Metrics
• Our Products and Service	• Challenges
• Features and Benefits	• Needs
• Technology	• Problems
• Price	• Opportunities
• Know-How	• Goals/Vision
• Our People, Skills and Capabilities	• Objectives
• Industry-Leading Solution	• Strategies
	• Performance
	• Change
	• Risk
	• Investment and Return

You should be concerned if you are using the seller-focused language on the left-hand-side of the previous table. However, if you find you are using the words on the right, it is a strong indicator that you are focused on the real needs of potential buyers.

The Challenge Of Uncovering Needs

So, what is so difficult about finding out about the buyer's needs before arriving at a solution?

Well here are some possible answers:

- The buyer is reluctant to reveal the full details of their problem to the seller.
- The buyer tells the salesperson what is wanted and the seller accepts it on face value.
- The salesperson does not have the knowledge or confidence to uncover the buyer's needs.
- The problem is obvious to the salesperson so getting straight to the solution makes sense.
- The seller assumes that the buyer can join the dots and link the solution to their problem.
- The seller believes blindly that their solution is the best regardless of the specific needs of the customer.
- Time with the buyer is limited so communicating key product information is a priority.
- The salesperson is selling at the wrong level (i.e. too low down) or selling to the wrong organization.

How To Meet The Buyer's Needs

You have 'the ideal solution' and you cannot wait to tell the buyer about it. Don't! You will get your chance later, first you must focus on what the buyer wants to achieve. You must address the buyer's needs first and only then offer solutions.

If a salesperson wants to sell their solution they must clearly demonstrate how it can solve the buyer's needs. The problem is that listing product features and benefits is an ineffective way of doing this.

To remedy this problem here is a checklist to guide you in identifying and then meeting the needs of the buyer:

1. **Avoid premature diagnosis of the problem.** Don't make assumptions regarding the customer's needs or assume they need what you are offering. Ask first and give the customer a chance to say no.

2. The expert may immediately know the problem and perhaps even the solution. However, they must **take care to involve the customer** in the discovery and build trust along the way. Connecting with buyer's needs requires a consultative approach with the salesperson adopting the role of an expert or trusted advisor.

3. **Understand what stage** the buyers is at:
   - The need is hidden (blissful ignorance)?
   - The need is recognized?
   - A budget has been set?
   - They are actively looking to resolve the need?

4. **Understand the company and its industry**, as well as its goals and strategy. Without this the seller will struggle to grasp what is motivating the buyer. Recognize the tradeoffs, constraints and complicating factors that bear on the needs. Understand needs from the perspective of the different stakeholders.

5. **Don't take the buyer's needs at face value.** Dig beneath the surface. Look to the implications of the needs. Help the buyer to develop a clearer picture of their needs and the advantages of solving them.

6. **Clarify the language and terms used** and what they mean to both parties. For example, simple terms such as 'process re-engineering' or 'stock accuracy' can have different meanings to different parties.

7. **More questions are not the answer.** Ask better questions that relate to needs and their implications.

8. **Buyers can be slow to open up.** Earn the right to ask questions by showing tact, and a willingness and ability to help.

9. **Be tactful and sensitive** regarding how you unearth the buyer's needs. Protect the person when identifying the problem and don't make the buyer feel like a fool.

10. **It is not enough just to listen** and understand needs, but to probe, inspire, enthuse and engage with the buyer around the opportunities and challenges facing their business.

11. **The salesperson must help the buyer envision life** after the problem has been solved. They must help them develop a clear vision regarding the business impact. Tact is required in highlighting buyer problems and challenges as there are likely to be sensitivities.

12. **Sell to those with latent needs.** The role of the salesperson now includes demand generation. That means traditional prequalification criteria (budget, authority, needs and timing) no longer apply.

13. **Sell higher in the organization.** This after all is where priorities and budgets are set in response to the identification of needs. This will require a new vocabulary and a new message. It also requires confidence and skill.

Asking The Right Questions

We made a note overleaf of some of the best questions salespeople employ to really understand the needs of the buyer. Which ones are most relevant to you and your team?

1. What do you (the buyer) <u>want to achieve</u>? What does the company want to achieve? What are the key business drivers in this area?

2. What is the <u>underlying opportunity or challenge</u> facing the business? How big is it? How urgent is it?

3. <u>What is the gap</u> between desired and actual performance in the area in question? How does this compare with internal and external expectations or benchmarks?

4. What are the relevant industry <u>drivers or trends?</u>

5. Are there any critical events or dates?

6. <u>Who does it impact on</u> most? How? Who else is affected? In what ways? What are the consequences? What is the cost?

7. What is the <u>impact on the business</u>? Has it been quantified? What are the benefits of its resolution? Are they quantified in a credible manner?

8. What are the relevant <u>metrics</u>? How will success be measured?

9. What is the impact on the businesses <u>goals and strategies</u>?

10. Is this area a <u>priority</u>? If it is why has it not been addressed to date? What have been the constraints? Has this issue been discussed in the past? What has happened as a result?

11. What are the <u>competing</u> priorities and projects?

12. Who are the various <u>stakeholders</u>?

13. How does it fit with existing <u>people and processes</u>?

14. What are the <u>barriers</u> to addressing the need/exploiting the opportunity? What could prevent it? What is the context in terms of the organizations history, culture, politics and strategy?

6. Think Total Solution

Everyday salespeople are forced to make assumptions regarding what buyers want. This is particularly the case where buyers  choose to keep sellers at arms length. When it comes to competitive bidding situations, sellers are forced to take the buyer's requirements at face value. However, it is vital the seller arrives at the solution in tandem with the buyer. The process must be based on a full and thorough exploration of needs and based on a joint assessment of alternatives.

Six Ways Sellers Misjudge The Solution

Not surprisingly sellers are very good at talking about their solutions, after all they know the features and benefits of their products and services off by heart. However, there can be a surprising difference between the seller's view of the solution and that of the buyer. Here are the top five reasons this divergence in viewpoints can occur:

1. The Salesperson Can't See The Alternatives

The buyer has a range of alternative solutions beyond that of the seller. Being aware of these alternatives is important in order to prevent surprises.

2. Confusion About The Source of Value

The buyer and seller can have a different view of the features and benefits that are most important. So, when sellers list off features and benefits they should stop to ask the buyer which ones are important and which ones are not. It is also important to remember buyers have a habit of changing their minds as they go through their own process, so it is worth making sure you have the most up-to-date perspective on what is and isn't important.

3. Key Success Factors Are Not Clear

The buyer knows that when it comes to meeting his organization's business needs the solution offered by the salesperson is only one element of success. In particular, there is a people and a process dimension to the buyer's overall solution.

> **BUYER INSIGHT**
>
> **The People, Process and Product Dimensions**
>
> 'Our public sector organization was shopping for the latest document management and file access solution. We knew that the success of the solution depended less on how good it was and more on how well we could implement it. In particular we were concerned to ensure it would fit with the people and processes already in place. In particular user adoption was going to be key.
>
> We chose the vendor that seemed to most appreciate the importance of implementation. As part of their response they outlined a program of training and support to users, process re-engineering and so on. The solution is never just about the selected product; it is a mix of product, people and process. We need confidence in all three.'
>
> Chief Secretary, Government Department

4. The Total Project View

The seller's solution is often only one element of an overall program or investment by the buyer. For example, one of our clients was negotiating the sale of its financial services solution, valued at almost €8 million, as part of a larger €120 million project within a financial institution. Knowing where their solution fitted into the complex project resulted in:

- Opportunities to run certain phases of the project concurrently, eliminating areas of overlap and offering the potential to share

resources (in respect of testing, for example) across a number of phases of the project.
- Having an appreciation of business drivers, constraints and the dependencies for the project overall.
- Understanding how other aspects of the project could impact on the success of the seller's implementation.
- Identifying a number of project partners (e.g. the consulting house) with whom relationships should be developed.

So, it is vital to know how your solution fits into the entire budget, program and strategy of the buyer.

5. Confusion About Scope

Lately we have been advising clients to include a new section in their proposals and executive briefing documents, that clearly spells out how both parties will know when the project is complete. That is a clearly defined outline of the scope of the project.

Solution scope is very important and sometimes overlooked particularly where:

- The scope of the project has not been clearly defined.
- The buyer's needs change during the course of the project resulting in scope creep.
- The demands of the project are seen to be different to those evident before project commencement when less information was to hand.

Salespeople can be tempted to promise the world when looking to close a deal. So, agreeing what is inside and outside of the scope is crucial not only for delivery, but also for project profitability, customer satisfaction, repeat selling and commission payments.

6. Confusion About The Expected Results

Buyers buy solutions because they want results. But sellers may not have a clear picture of what exactly those results are. As examined in the section **First Needs, Then Solutions**, sellers need to help customers model the results expected.

7. Review Early & Often

Forecasting what deals will close and when is more difficult than ever. This is because of the more complex buying processes and,

of course, more uncertain market conditions. Reviewing all opportunities early and often is a vital task.

Get That 'No' Early On

The more time a salesperson has invested in a sales cycle the more determined they become the deal will close. But they can become blind to signals that suggest the buyer is not as keen as they might want to believe.

By nature a salesperson must be optimistic. But that can result in a reluctance to hear no for an answer. However, hearing no is not a problem if it comes early in the cycle and before the salesperson has spent too much time in meetings and preparing proposals. Salespeople must therefore make it easy for the customer to say no at each stage of the sales process.

As mentioned earlier, that 'no' can take a number of forms, such as 'no, not quite', 'no, not at all' or 'no, not at this time'. It will either redirect your efforts towards a yes or point you in the direction of finding potential customers elsewhere. Either way, getting a 'yes' or 'no' will ultimately mean you are better off. It means you can ensure that you are not wasting either your time or that of the buyer.

Take Away Your Solution

You have been selling your solution to the customer and suddenly you realize they may not be as eager as you first thought. In order to put their commitment to the test you can use one of the following questions:

- There seems to be a lot happening in your company at the moment so perhaps there are more immediate priorities?
- Maybe the problem is not as great or as urgent as I thought?
- Maybe this is not the right time for you to be making this decision?
- Perhaps a different approach would suit your business?

The reaction will either be, 'Yes, I think you are right' and it is clear that it is time to move on, at least for now. But it could also be, 'No, we definitely need your solution', or some version of this.

Why Getting An Answer Is Important

Buyers sometimes don't appreciate what they are getting until it is taken away. They can happily sit back and leave the salesperson do all the running. So being put on the spot by having the solution taken away can be an effective way to help buyers quickly clarify what is important and what is not.

In an ideal world buyers would always tell you what they are really thinking, but as we all know this is not the case. All too often buyers are reluctant to 'burst your bubble' and will likely let you continue chasing the bone until you finally give up and go away of your own accord.

Another approach has a similar effect in terms of measuring the head of steam built up behind a sale — presenting the legal documentation concerning the sale to your sponsor and waiting to see what is said. The buyer will either say, 'I will pass them on to my colleague', or that 'it is too early for legal documents at this stage'. Hey presto — you have instant insight into the likelihood and timing of a sale.

Reviewing The Pipeline

The age of the 'lone ranger' salesperson is, by necessity, at an end. Selling to multi-functional buying teams requires a pairing of executives on both sides. The pipeline review is an ideal opportunity to coordinate and orchestrate the efforts of your entire organization in the advancement of pipeline opportunities.

The way in which most pipeline reviews are conducted means salespeople can be reluctant to reduce the probability figure of an opportunity or discuss areas of concern. This is particularly true where reviews are infrequent or take place late in the sales cycle.

It is the easiest thing in the world to tear somebody's pipeline apart, asking all the questions and second-guessing all the answers. Managers must take greater care in managing opportunity reviews ensuring the focus is kept on the sales pipeline, the prospect's buying process and not the salesperson. These reviews must be positive and forward-looking.

Review Checklist

Based on how account reviews are managed in more than 120 companies here is a checklist of ways to ensure their effectiveness:

(a) Organization And Timing

1. **Conduct opportunity reviews early and often**. Most important opportunities should be reviewed every four weeks. The trickiest reviews are those that are left till late in the cycle when the room to manoeuver and appetite for re-appraisal is severely limited.
2. **Don't try to discuss too many opportunities at once**. What usually happens is those first on the list get lots of discussion, with those left till the end receiving only a cursory review.

3. **Conduct reviews outside of the sales meeting** and avoid them in large groups (unless there has been a one-to-one review with the opportunity owner first).

4. **To be effective, the sales manager must act in the role of coach**. Before the review ends the manager should ask the salesperson questions such as: 'What help and support do you need?', 'What are your key goals and priorities?' and 'What opportunities do you see to improve the way we sell?'

5. **Focus the review on the business decision** that underpins the buying decision, paying attention to the goals, strategies and priorities of the buyer's business.

(b) The Tone Of The Review

6. **Review the account not the salesperson**. Where there are issues, depersonalize them by focusing on actions, techniques and process as opposed to pointing the finger at the salesperson.

7. **Ensure reviews are forward looking**. After all what is done is done and there is no point focusing on the past.

8. **Keep reviews positive**. Avoid apportioning blame. Use them as opportunities for learning. This is key to ensuring reviews are productive.

9. **Keep reviews realistic.** Ensure they challenge any assumptions being made. Look to identify any gaps in information, understanding of the buying process, and coverage of the buying unit or the rationale for making the business decision. Look out for early warning signals (see list overleaf).

10. **Make it easy to revisit and write down probabilities** and timing forecasts, if required. The person facilitating the review should prompt for a reappraisal of dates and probabilities, again with reference to sales process guidelines.

(c) Account Reviews Structure

11. **There should be an agreed structure for account reviews,** with key headings to be followed and preparation by participants in advance of the meeting.
12. **The organization's buyer-friendly sales process should be used as a guide.**
13. **Each review should be documented**, in particular its actions recapped and allocated an owner and completion date.
14. **Use the sales or CRM system** to guide the review, ensuring that the account details are up to date in advance of the session and updated with actions post the session.
15. **Use the business case headings** to review progress of the opportunity (costs, benefits, risk, compliance and strategic fit).

(d) Preparation In Advance Of The Review

16. **Prepare a one-page account review**, update the sales system (with notes of meetings, contact details, etc.) and review RSS feeds and other sources of information on the company and its industry.
17. **Co-ordinate with the various people** who have a knowledge of and involvement with the opportunity or the industry in question.
18. **Seek the advice of the sponsor** so the review reflects the buyer's perspective.

Can You Spot The Warning Signals?

Based on a review of hundreds of pipeline opportunities we have spotted some common **early warning signals** that an opportunity may be at risk. Use the list to review your top three sales opportunities. Tick the items that are relevant to the opportunity you are considering.

Don't have access to all the <u>stakeholders</u>. ☐

Don't have all the <u>information</u> needed. ☐

The same <u>issues</u> keep resurfacing repeatedly. ☐

Salesperson is doing all the <u>running</u> (buyer does not complete his actions). ☐

The buyer seems to be '<u>going along</u>' with everything you say. ☐

Meetings are getting postponed or <u>dates</u> put back. ☐

Delays, setbacks or <u>surprises</u> are happening. ☐

You hear conflicting <u>stories</u> from within the buying organization. ☐

Sudden internal <u>changes</u> (people, priorities, mergers/acquisition, etc.). ☐

The buyer's industry or market is in a state of <u>flux</u>, or turmoil. ☐

Last minute, or rushed changes in <u>requirements</u> and specifications. ☐

Price issues arise <u>too early</u> (e.g. before requirements/scope has been set). ☐

The temperature of the <u>relationship</u> appears to have suddenly changed. ☐

There are <u>political</u> or personality issues in the buying organization. ☐

<u>Credibility</u> questions are continually being asked about your company. ☐

You don't have a <u>champion</u>/coach in the buying organization. ☐

You don't feel sufficiently <u>respected</u> (e.g. buyer is late for meetings). ☐

<u>Another supplier</u> has a strong existing, or past relationship with the buyer. ☐

Your gut <u>instinct</u> tells you something 'is off'. ☐

The <u>business case</u> is weak, absent, or kept from sight. ☐

There are <u>competing projects</u> vying for the same budget. ☐

The Sales Cycles Revolution — A Summary

The area of greatest opportunity for improvement in respect of win rates is not in terms of the proposal or the closing, but the process that leads up to it. That is the process of engagement between buyer and seller around needs and solutions. It is where the buyer stops selling and focuses on helping the buyer to buy in a total of seven different ways:

SALES
THE CYCLES
REVOLUTION

1. **Think buying process, not sales process.** The seller has to put aside his idealized notions of the sales process, in order to help the buyer to navigate the increasingly rigorous and sophisticated process that he or she must follow.

2. **Business decision, not buying decision.** The seller's competitive advantage or value proposition won't convince the buyer to buy, unless the fundamental business logic for buying has been established. So sellers need to connect with what buyers are trying to achieve — the strategies, the priorities and the payback required.

3. **To speed up, slow down.** Sales cycles are getting longer and that makes the seller impatient for a decision. However, if the seller attempts to accelerate the sale, while key steps of the buying process or business decision are outstanding, a positive outcome is highly unlikely.

4. **Access is a privilege, not a right.** The salesperson, once the ringmaster of the sale, often feels as if they are on the outside looking in. Accessing decision makers, particularly at C level is a key challenge, engaging with them is even more challenging still.

5. **First Needs, then solutions.** It can be tempting to immediately present the buyer with a solution, but don't. Most sellers should spend up to nine times more time talking about what the buyer is trying to achieve than the features or benefits of the solution they are selling.

6. **Think Total Solution.** Sellers know their solutions inside out, but that means they can make dangerous assumptions regarding what buyers see as the ideal solution. The process by which buyer and seller explore solutions to arrive at the ideal is paramount.

7. **Review Early And Often.** Any opportunity is only as good as its last review, however painful that review is. If sellers follow the steps outlined and review opportunities earlier and more often then many of the surprises and disappointments that arise can be avoided.

By following the above rules for sales cycles the seller will have helped to build a relationship of trust and respect. They will have engaged with the buyer in matching needs and solutions and explored the fundamental business logic of the decision. Thus, with the sales cycle effectively managed, then the seller is ideally positioned to successfully propose, negotiate and close the sales order. These steps are examined in the next Section — Revolutionizing Sales Orders.

SECTION 10:

The Sales Orders Revolution

THE NEW RULES FOR CLOSING

Traditionally salespeople have relied on sales proposals, closing methods and negotiating techniques to conclude the sale. However, in the face of growing buyer power and sophistication, these outdated closing techniques are more likely to close the door than the sale.

The reality is that the traditional sales proposal, closing technique and negotiating stance have been rendered impotent. They are blunt instruments when it comes to getting major purchases sanctioned. The unsophisticated sales proposal needs to undergo a revolution. Its role, audience and message need to be transformed.

Traditionally sales proposals were:

- Written by salespeople to entice their selection by the buyer.
- Aimed at a technical, or middle management audience.
- Focused predominately on features, benefits and price.
- Prepared at the end of the sales process.

However, because they were written with little input from the buyer, they often contained surprises that only revealed themselves when presented for sign off.

The Changing Role Of The Proposal

Sales success now requires a radically transformed sales proposal. New proposals are not about confirming supplier selection, but justifying the business decision. Their audience is senior management, thus they focus on detailing the business case and the expected return on investment.

Sales proposals are no longer left until the end of the sales cycle but rather evolve throughout the process. To ensure the final document contains no surprises for either party they must be written as a joint effort involving both buyer and salesperson.

The New Rules For Sales Orders

Sellers can vastly improve their success rate by adopting a collaborative approach to the development of the sales proposal throughout the sales cycle. That involves obeying the following rules:

1. Business Case Before Proposal.
2. Proposals, Without Surprises.
3. Business Impact, Not Benefits.
4. Write The Last Page First.
5. Think Risk and Insurance.
6. Walk If You Cannot Talk.
7. Close With Care.
8. Wish Them Well.

1. BUSINESS CASE BEFORE PROPOSAL

Understandably, sellers feel helpless and frustrated when confronted with surprise buyer u-turns or stalled buying decisions. Their traditional sales proposals, closing techniques and negotiating stances don't help. Indeed, they are often a part of the problem.

Preventing Surprises And Setbacks

A sales proposal, no matter how well written, won't get a major purchase sanctioned. Only a compelling business case can do that.

Big projects don't stall because the buyer cannot select a supplier. They stall because they lack a compelling business case. Quite simply, if the business imperative has not been established there is nothing the sales proposal can do about it.

Most selling focuses on the sales proposal and fails to recognize:

- The key challenge facing the buyer is not to select a supplier, but to get the go ahead for their project.
- The real competition is not a competing supplier, but a decision to delay a decision, to do it in-house or support a competing project.

The most powerful way for a seller to demonstrate their value to a buyer and differentiate themselves from competitors is to underpin the business logic of the project.

Sales Proposals Don't Get Projects Approved

Most sales proposals do not address the fundamental question every buyer needs answered — 'How is this purchase going to increase the performance of my business?' Therefore they don't provide the key information required in order to get a purchase approved.

Take, for example, the structure of the typical vendor proposal, compared to the structure of the buyer's business case or purchase approvals document.

The typical salesperson proposal focuses on the following key headings:

- Problem
- Solution
- Benefits/Features
- Cost
- Team, Company and Credentials

However, this is out of sync with the structure of the buyer's business case, which requires information under the following key headings:

- Strategic Rationale
- Economic Analysis — Costs/Benefits
- Risk Analysis
- Recommendation
- Implementation

Little wonder then that seller's proposals are missing the mark.

As we examined in **Part 1** the buyers thought process around buying is a sophisticated one:

The problem is that the sales proposal is not as sophisticated. Indeed, it often neglects key issues that can result in a 'go', or 'no go' buying decision. As examined in Section 3 of Part 1 these economic, strategic, risk and political issues are the key components of the business case.

The Compelling Business Case

Sellers who write fancy proposals promoting their so-called unique advantages over other suppliers entirely miss the point. The focus has to be on jointly developing a compelling business case with your sponsor within the buying organization. The purchasing decision will only be sanctioned when the sponsor can convince senior management the purchase will further the objectives and strategies of the business.

The word 'compelling' is key because in these difficult times only those projects that stand head and shoulders above the rest will succeed.

In an era of stalled projects and slashed budgets, choosing between the comparative advantages of different suppliers takes second place to justifying the project and getting it sanctioned internally — the role of the business case. The winning business case must therefore address the priorities of the business. It must deliver results and fast.

The B2B Revolution | Section 10

Meeting The Challenge

Writing sales proposals can be relatively easy, but shaping the buyer's business case is far more difficult. Creating a compelling proposition requires a lot more information, analysis and consultation.

Even if the seller could present the buyer with a completed business case it would miss the fundamental point of taking a collaborative approach. To ensure the business case succeeds requires consultation with a wide array of stakeholders within the buying organization who have to be involved in the process of its creation.

Even during the initial encounter the sellers must focus on the business case by talking about the results achieved by other customers. It is vital to put the essential business case equation ((benefits − costs) x risk) at the forefront of the sales proposal, as well as during the subsequent negotiation and closing.

Throughout the sales process the seller must provide the buyer with information that can either directly or indirectly influence the business case. That means providing case studies, whitepapers, success stories and insights instead of traditional off-the-shelf marketing collateral and proposal templates.

How To Influence The Business Case

Sellers will rarely get to write the buyer's business case. But they must influence the hand of the buyer or buying group in developing it. That requires the following vital ingredients — the right information, focus, numbers and process.

1. The Right Information

- Communicate the business results achieved by others — right from the first point of contact.
- Provide validated data from previous customers and analysts.
- Ensure the buyer has an opportunity to:
  - Access your experts.
  - Learn from your customers.
- Provide the buyer with useful information, such as technical whitepapers containing expert information. Remember, buyers cannot use marketing blurb in their business cases.

2. The Right Focus

- Help the buyer compare and contrast alternatives — the business case must show why the proposed route is better than others available.
- Help the buyer to comprehensively address issues that sometimes get overlooked:
  - Risks, including how they can be mitigated.
  - Constraints that may impact on the project.
  - Competing projects — help the buyer to demonstrate how the project is consistent with corporate goals and strategies.
  - Complicating factors, such as politics or conflicting priorities.
  - Strategic fit — how the project connects to organizational goals.

3. The Right Numbers

- Ensure that your calculations of the benefits/results of your solution are both credible and compelling.
- Use the same metrics that are important to the buyer and focus continually on results.

- Help the buyer to quantify the impact of your solution (including the ROI) using a model with which they are comfortable (this is discussed in more detail later).
- Help the buyer to validate and test assumptions and scenarios used in establishing the business case, in particular with reference to external benchmarks.

4. The Right Process

- Act as a sounding board. Share lessons learned from other customers when securing business case approval.
- Provide templates, tools and other material that can assist the buyer in preparing the business case.
- Help facilitate the consultation process with stakeholders (e.g. workshops on requirements).
- Assist in the process of requirements definition, project planning and technical analysis.
- Help the buyer prepare the business case documentation, including drafting elements of inclusion, providing source information from which the buyer can draw, providing tools and templates (e.g. models, diagrams).
- Help the buyer prepare to present the project for review. For example, adopt the role of devil's advocate, helping the buyer to prepare for questions that may arise when they are presenting to their buying steering committee.

2. PROPOSALS, WITHOUT SURPRISES

In an ideal world the salesperson's proposal would be greeted with a 'that is exactly what we want' from the buyer. However, most proposals fail to reflect the real needs of buyers, because they are based on so much guesswork.

The Proposal Guessing Game

Sometimes buyers and sellers can be reluctant to spend the time required to get to know each other and work jointly on the alignment of needs and solutions. For example:

- The seller, motivated to accelerate the sale, may rush to prepare a proposal, short-circuiting the often time consuming process of interaction with the buyer.
- The buyer, in a desire to ensure buying procedures and a competitive bidding process is followed, may limit interaction with the seller.

Sometimes, instead of sending a salesperson, the vendor sends a proposal. Interaction is replaced with paperwork, presumption and guesswork. However, the exchange of paper is no substitute for the exchange of ideas, alternatives and knowledge between buyer and seller.

Without sufficient interaction between buyer and seller a mismatch of needs and solutions is inevitable. The seller never gets the opportunity to thoroughly explore the buyer's needs or how they fit with various solution alternatives and as a result they make ill-informed assumptions about what is necessary.

This also impacts negatively on the buyer: If the definition of needs remains constant from start to finish of the buying process and remains untouched as a result of seller interaction, the buyer runs a great risk of making a sub-optimal choice.

SELLER INSIGHT

'It is a poor sales person that cannot cast a new angle on the buyer's needs. After all we should have witnessed many such similar situations and should have developed insights that are not available to the buyer.'

EMEA Sales Director BPO Vendor

The Seller Proposes, The Buyer Disposes

The traditional sales proposal is a logical but flawed end to a sales process based on pitches and presentations.

Salespeople too often take the buyer's declared needs at face value and make assumptions in order to fill the gaps. The 'sales proposal' then becomes a 'surprise proposal'.

The first to be surprised by this approach is the buyer who receives a proposal that does not meet their needs. This in turn leads to a surprised salesperson left struggling to understand why the buyer has suddenly disappeared and won't return calls.

Sales Proposals, Not Surprise Proposals

Let us be clear — proposals don't sell (or at least not very well). The selling, and by selling we mean consultative selling, has to take place before the proposal is prepared.

Yet proposals are used to try and sell everyday. Indeed, the rise of the RFP (Request For Proposal) has made the sales proposal created in a vacuum even more common. This results in surprise, frustration and misunderstanding for buyer and seller alike.

The reality is that a sales proposal can never take the place of time spent listening to the buyer and the resulting two-way exchange of ideas and building of rapport. So, it is not just the sales proposal that needs to be re-imagined, but all the steps in the buying and selling process.

The key questions that need to be asked before sending a proposal are:

- Do we have enough information?
- Do we fully understand what the buyer is trying to achieve and all the issues, constraints, nuances and inherent risks?
- Has there been sufficient interaction with the buyer?
- Has there been sufficient access to and engagement with the buyer to ensure they own the solution?
- How will the buying company's board feel about this type of investment?

Confirm Before You Propose

Successful sales professionals don't leave the selling to the proposal. They simply use it as a tool to document what has been explored, discussed and agreed throughout the sales cycle.

The effective sales proposal:

- Results from the interaction between buyer and seller, not from a word processor or template.
- Is not written by a salesperson locked away in a room, but shaped by every interaction, every meeting and conversation with the buying team.

- Represents the culmination of a two-way exchange of ideas, discussion of requirements, exploration of options and discussion of impact.
- Is used to document what has already been discussed and in large measure agreed.

That is not to say that buyer and seller need to dictate paragraphs each time they interact. It does, however, require an ongoing process of examining alternatives and scoping solutions throughout the sales cycle.

Selling is not an individual sport and not about the buyer and seller competing. It's about the buyer and seller being on the same team.

As a result, the compelling message contained within the sales proposal is not 'this is what we (the seller) recommend,' but rather 'this is what we (buyer and seller) have agreed and discussed.'

When the buyers ask, 'How can we do this?' the ownership of the solution has passed from the seller and the process of interaction has been successful. It is then time to write a proposal together.

SELLER INSIGHT

'To deliver a compelling business case to the client means that the cost of the sale is rising day-by-day. I had one opportunity on our sales system for over 300 days with ongoing interaction and yet no sale. Even when the initial order did come it was small.

However, within a year they have now grown to one of our largest and most loyal customers. My colleagues — who chided me for wasting my time — are slowly coming around to my way of thinking: you really do have to stay the course and invest for the long term.'

Salesperson – Global Logistics Technology Company

3. BUSINESS IMPACT, NOT BENEFITS

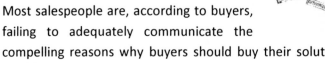

Most salespeople are, according to buyers, failing to adequately communicate the compelling reasons why buyers should buy their solutions. It is time for sellers to put their 'benefits pitch' on steroids and provide buyers with the metrics, quantification and validation that is required.

What Buyers Need To Hear

Salespeople need to stop explaining why their solution is so great and instead show each buyer in turn how their business will be better as a result. This must be backed up by real figures and real customer stories.

Sellers who rely on benefits to sell are not telling buyers what they want to hear. As a result they end up having the wrong conversations at the wrong levels with inevitable consequences on their sales success.

The problem with benefits is that they are rarely compelling. Indeed, as the table overleaf shows, traditional seller benefits are firecrackers, while business impact is dynamite.

Most benefits are not worthy of discussion at the board table, because they rarely impact on the bottom line, at least not tangibly. Once more they are often confused with features and with competitors. The opposite is true of business impact.

	OLD: BENEFITS	NEW: BUSINESS IMPACT
Buyer Reaction:	• 'So What!?'	• 'Tell Me More'
Quantified:	• No	• Yes, Clear Metrics
Validation:	• None, Supplier Says So	• Proven By Customers
Focused on:	• Value Proposition	• Buyer's Key Metrics
Relevant to:	• 'Technical' Buyers	• Senior Management
Uniqueness:	• Similar To Others	• Stands-Out
Contained in:	• Marketing Brochures	• Customer Case Studies
Used in:	• Seller Sales Pitches	• Buyer Business Case

BUYER INSIGHT

The Supplier That 'Stood Out From The Crowd'

B

'After reviewing tender responses from more than a dozen companies, we struggled to distinguish one from the other. After all, their features and benefits had an uncanny sameness. Only one vendor stood apart from rest — it had quantified statements of the results attested to by other high-profile customers. Using the limited data provided by us, the seller had presented a number of scenarios and had asked for the opportunity to input to a more robust business model. We are very focused on results and it appeared to us that this particular supplier was similarly focused.'

Manager – Fortune 500 Pharmaceutical Company

Benefits Out, Business Impact In

Buyers want to talk results and little else. This is the reason they are sitting up and paying attention to those sellers who quantify results and back it up with third-party validation. All those sellers who rely on the adjectives and slogans provided by their marketing department are putting buyers to sleep.

Buyers want the answers that cannot be found in traditional marketing literature or sales aides. They want metrics, not slogans. They want quantifiable data, not marketing adjectives. They want solid statements of business impact, not fluffy benefits and features presentations.

To put it another way, buyers want something that merits talking about at the board table. Yet, most vendors don't get it. Telling buyers that the solution is '24X7', 'meets health and safety access requirements,' is 'SOA enabled' or meets a 'waste emissions standard' falls short of the compelling reason required to make the purchasing decision.

Buyers want something they can put in a spreadsheet and see translated into a future revenue, profit or asset value projections. That means they need numbers, not adjectives. They also want to understand the impact on their own personal recognition within the organization. People will often stick their heads out to get a decision through if they think it will help their careers. Many salespeople fail to understand how a successful purchasing decision will impact on their sponsor's career or bonus plan, even though this can play a major role in committing them to your solution.

Business Impact

Is your benefit statement compelling enough to communicate to the business case? Take the test:

- Does it communicate the results to be achieved? ☐
- Is it quantified? Can you put numbers on it? ☐
- Does it enable a before and after comparison? ☐
- Does it relate to the key metrics used by senior managers? ☐
- Does it relate to the performance of the buyer's business? ☐
- Does it connect with the buyer's priorities and strategies? ☐

- Is it worthy of discussion at board level or among senior managers? ☐
- It is believable? ☐
- Can it be validated by customers or others? ☐

BUYER INSIGHT

'Very few salespeople want to help me cut costs or do more for less. They want a bigger slice of my budget, which incidentally is getting smaller. But why should I help them meet their target, if they can't help me meet my own.'

Group Purchasing Manager Tier 1 Bank

Communicating Business Impact

Sellers need to find an unambiguous and compelling way to communicate the reason for buying their solutions. That means the seller must be able to present a before and after picture in terms of the impact of their solution. For example: 'Before our solution was implemented, the customer faced key challenges meaning they could only achieve X results. Then, after our solution was employed the customer overcame many of these challenges and achieved Y results.

Thus the net improvement in results was Z (that is Y-X).'

As the diagram suggests sellers must understand what results are most important in the context of key business and industry drivers. They therefore must understand the businesses priorities, goals and strategies, as well as the industry context in terms of opportunities, challenges and events in its industry. This is evident from the metrics used in the example below.

Customer A, Results Achieved	Before	After	Change
Admin cost per policy	18	12	-33%
Time to Issue New Policy (days)	4	1	-75%
Cost of handling customer enquiry	3	1.5	-50%
Cost of policy amendment	4	2	-50%
New Policies Issued Weekily	2000	2200	10%
Enquiry to Policy Win Rate	50%	55%	10%
Time to market for new products (weeks)	6	2	-67%

What is important to managers? Well, clearly results! But how performance is measured will vary for managers at different levels, with different job titles and in different industries. The seller must understand the specific performance metrics that are relevant for the buying organization overall, as well as for the different buyer-managers and stakeholders.

Know What Metrics Matter

At board level the key metrics are found in the balance sheet, the profit and loss account and the strategic business plan. When it comes to managers and their departments, the key metrics of interest can vary greatly, depending for example on whether it is the COO or the CIO. However, it is important that the seller knows specifically which performance metrics matter and to whom.

Sellers often shy away from talking about results because they know as soon as they use metrics buyers will want to know who else achieved such results and how these results were achieved. Ultimately, they will also want to see the data to back-up such metrics and a robust model that can be applied in their own business to calculate impact. However, almost all vendors will struggle to produce the data to support such models because, as we will discuss later, they simply do not have the insight and data from previous customer engagements.

Why Salespeople Struggle With Business Impact

Why do sellers find it so difficult to talk about business impact? Well, we asked them and here are some of the main reasons:

- 'We **don't have enough information on the results achieved** by other customers using our solutions.' Without the tools required — that is the models, the case studies and references — they must rely on the traditional benefits and features message.
- 'We are **not talking to the right people**' — they only have access to lower ranks who are typically more focused on the detail (technology, features, etc.) and less concerned with the big picture.

- 'We are **talking to the right people, but about the wrong thing**' — they are slowly coming to realize that their traditional benefits and features message is no longer of interest to senior managers.
- '**It is a good idea in principle, but in practice it does not work**'. This exists where the following factors are wrongly considered to prevent using numbers to sell:
    - 'Every company is different.'
    - 'Many of the benefits we sell are intangible.'
    - 'There are many other variables at play.'

- '**Buyers are weary of our claims** and getting them to open up about figures can prove difficult.' The two issues involved are confidentiality and credibility — points that will be discussed later.
- 'We are uncomfortable **dealing with numbers, spreadsheets and ROI calculations**.' That means a crash course in dealing with numbers is required.

4. WRITE THE LAST PAGE FIRST

Have you ever noticed buyers have an infuriating habit of starting to read from the back, as opposed to the front of the sales proposal? They want numbers. This is something that sellers often underestimate.

Most vendor proposals are shy on metrics — at least the key metrics of interest to senior managers. Indeed, often the only quantifiable data relates to cost. The last few pages of the sales proposal sheepishly deliver a price tag and that is it.

Sellers know that buyers must justify the purchase in terms of an increasingly sophisticated cost-benefit equation. However, they are prepared to rely on buyers to do the math to arrive at the right answer.

Sellers' proposals should provide a robust justification of the investment that is required on the part of the buyer. They must put the ROI on the first page of their proposals in a prominent position in the executive summary. However, they have to take care that buyers have bought into their figures — something that can present challenges.

Why Buyers Don't Believe Vendor ROI Models

We asked buyers about the role of the vendor in helping to build the economic justification for their purchases. The response was somewhat contradictory. While they want to see an ROI model from the salesperson, they are unlikely to believe or use them.

Through our research we have highlighted ten reasons why buyers are hesitant in talking numbers with vendors:

1. **We have our own model** — 'There is an in-house format that we must adhere to'.

2. **Our business is different** — 'That model is more suited to other companies.'

3. **It is too complex** — 'There are too many sheets, too many calculations, too many assumptions, etc.'

4. **It is lacking in objectivity** — 'If the board thought data was being provided by the vendor it would raise a lot of questions'.

5. **The assumptions made are rarely verified** — 'You have put the efficiency gain at 50%, but what is that based on?' or 'I could not stand over the data if asked to by my board' or 'Is that backed up by research or by your customers?'

6. **The total cost of ownership is not considered** — 'OK, you put the cost at $1.5 million, but that is just your charges, there will be a lot more cost on our side'.

7. **It is presented as a 'fait accompli'** — 'If we are not involved in creating the model, then we don't own it'. Implication: the process is as important as the output.

8. **It is confidential** — 'We cannot share that information because it is confidential to our business.'

9. **It is used by the salesperson to justify price**, or at least set expectations regarding cost.

10. **The salesperson is not the right person** to talk to about numbers — 'I cannot imagine the salesperson being able to talk about investment analysis with our CFO.'

> BUYER INSIGHT
>
> 'We have our own models — sophisticated models with calculations that reflect our internal financial rules **B** and the weighting that reflect our priorities and our past experience of other projects. We cannot put them aside in favor of the seller's model even if we wanted to.'
>
> Buyer Multinational Technology Company

More Credible Seller Metrics

If salespeople want buyers to value and use the figures provided in the sales proposal a better approach is required. In particular, sales professionals require new tools, approaches and skills.

(a) New Tools

- Salespeople need an easy-to-use and credible tool to calculate ROI and other key metrics that will help buyers explore the impact the solution will have on their business. However, they also need customer case studies, references, whitepapers and industry data to back up the figures they provide.
- It is not about creating the perfect tool, but a series of models suited to different types of customers and industries.
- The models must be tailored in terms of levels of detail to reflect different stages of the sales cycle.
- At the start of the buying process/sales cycle the model is likely to use standard industry figures or benchmarks and be based on the results typically achieved by other customers.
- As the buying process progresses the information will be tailored to the specifics of the customer's business.
- The model should be validated by the seller's CFO, as well as by reference to industry experts, customers and analysts.

(b) A New Approach

- Sellers must show their interest in numbers by talking about metrics right from the initial sales meeting. That means starting by detailing the results achieved by other customers. If the business case conversation is left until the sales cycle is advanced, then there is the risk it will take place without the salesperson being involved.
- It is essential to develop the model in a consultative manner in order to ensure the accuracy and relevance of the model, as

well as to ensure buy-in on the part of the buyer. Presenting the buyer with a completed model simply won't work.

- The seller must coach the buyer through the completion of the model, developing scenarios and options from which the buyer can choose, or at a minimum providing industry benchmarking and other data the buyer can use. Unless the buyer has been involved in creating the model they most likely won't be willing or able to defend it in front of others.

- Obviously, the seller needs the trust of the buyer if a conversation about numbers is to take place. The salesperson must also show they are careful with other customer's information.

(c) New Skills

Salespeople have to get better with numbers. They must be able to confidently and credibly talk about ROI, ARR, IRR and so on. They must be coached by their CFO in the language and the methodology of the business case and investment decision.

However, trying to turn a salesperson into a financial analyst does not make sense. Sales organizations must match the right person to the role of inputting data into the buyer's financial model as the sales process progresses.

Salespeople need to steep themselves in the business case and ROI model with the help of their colleagues in finance. This will help them get to grips with accounting terms, such as APR (Annual Percentage Rate), ARR (Accounting Rate of Return) and IRR (Internal Rate of Return), and help them to create a robust model to help buyers calculate the investment logic behind the solution being sold to them.

S

The operations director made a commitment to building a base of customer success stories, after realizing nothing captures buyer attention better than metrics. Now, at the start of every new project the project delivery manager is provided with a template to capture project data. This is an essential element in ensuring there is both 'before and after' data gathered for every project.

The data captured is the raw material needed to communicate the impact or success of the project. These metrics are key for two reasons: firstly, they help validate the ROI model agreed with the buyer at the outset of the project (helping to ensure repeat business); and secondly they give the sales team the metrics and data they need to open up conversations with other relevant contacts.

IT Services Company

5. Think Risk Insurance

To attempt to close the sale when all concerns have not been fully addressed is futile, perhaps even dangerous. In these risky times vendors must minimize risk and inspire trust in the process.

Risky Business

Buyer risk is something that must be carefully managed, particularly now that a decade of confidence and buoyant markets has come to an end. In a turbulent market, risk is the number one reason many projects and purchases are put on hold.

When confronted with risk and uncertainty buyers tend to make slower and more cautious decisions. This is something that was discussed in Section 3 of Part 1.

Traditionally risk has not been considered sufficiently in the management of the sales process or in proposal documentation. Sellers have tended to tippy-toe around risk and associated concerns, because they fear raising such issues may give them credence.

The seller needs to build confidence not just in the solution, but also to minimize risk and insure against failure.

Risk Sensitive Selling

While purchase decisions always hold the promise of success, they also carry the risk of failure. This risk comes under a number of headings:

1. Business risk

- Is the business model robust?
- Are assumptions tested?
- Are changes in the market considered?
- Is there market validation?

2. Project risk

- Has the project been planned sufficiently?
- Are there adequate controls in place?
- Have people and process issues been considered?

3. Supplier risk

- How stable is the supplier?
- If we choose them and they take another big client on board how will they be able to deliver?

4. Technology risk

- Is the technology risky?
- Is the implementation, integration or adoption going to be a challenge?

Despite what you may think, the choice of supplier is generally not the greatest risk in most projects. There are many other factors that may impinge on the achievement of the required outcome – as the questions above suggest.

So, the salesperson should not only be concerned about convincing the buyer the solution will deliver on its promises, but that the buyers will achieve the outcomes they expect.

All of the above risks should be of concern to the salesperson as they have the potential to stall or even scupper the sale. The modern salesperson needs to understand they are in the risk management business.

Managing Buyer Risk

Tackling the issue of supplier-related risk should be top of the agenda for the salesperson, as they need to ensure that the buyer feels their company is a safe choice. However, this can be a challenge as buyers can be slow to admit their concerns. If the sellers waits until a risk or concern is raised by the buyer it may be too late.

Sales teams have to be sensitive to buyer risk and must bring any concerns out into the open so that they can be addressed. That requires considerable skill. The seller must make it easy for the buyer to open up and admit that there are issues they are not comfortable with.

The seller must also anticipate and test for possible concerns. They can do this indirectly by saying things like: 'In other companies we have worked with managers had concerns about how their internal IT operations would react to the use of outside contractors. Is this something that you have thought about?'

BUYER INSIGHT

The salesperson was in pole position. Their solution represented the closest match to the buyer's requirements and had a clear technical advantage.
From the feedback received, the sale seemed a 'sure thing'. However, as the decision neared, the buyer got a case of last minute jitters.

A member of the buying group raised the question of the vendor's track record and credibility. They posed the question — 'Why take a chance on a new company?' The deal quietly faded away.

The order went to a less innovative, but safer supplier in the eyes of the buyer. The buyer expressed regret, but reluctant to offend, merely cited price as the reason why the deal was lost.

Buyer anxieties can express themselves in any number of ways, many of which can easily be overlooked by the salesperson. For example, when the buyer repeatedly raises an issue that the seller feels has already been addressed. (The early warning signals that can indicate a sales cycle in trouble are listed in Section 4: Revolutionizing Sales Cycles under the heading '*Review Regularly and Often*'.)

Risks or concerns are often the result of a lack of information or misunderstanding. To minimize risk the following is important:

- Make sure you know the buying process and that you adhere to it fully – it is for the buyer a process designed to manage risk.
- Maintain a high level of interaction during the sales cycle and maintain your focus on the business case.
- Always confirm understanding as the sales cycle progresses. The following questions will help:
  o Have I captured your requirements fully?
  o Do you have any concerns that we have not discussed yet?
  o Is there anything that you feel may be missing?
  o Would other stakeholders agree with what we have presented?

Bringing Risk Out Into the Open

Bringing buyer concerns out into the open requires good communication and high levels of trust. In particular, it is important to give the buyer a safe setting in which concerns can be aired. They may prefer to do it off the record or one-to-one, such as on the fringe of a meeting (when the rest of the attendees have gone) or during a meal or social meeting. The seller has to explicitly ask the buyer about risk, albeit in a tactful and sensitive way. Some key questions about risk include:

- What would you see as the risks associated with this project?
- Have any risks been overlooked, underestimated or exaggerated?

- What do you feel could prevent the project being a success?
- How confident are you about what has been forecasted?
- Could this project face any internal hurdles or resistance in terms of approval or implementation?
- Has this been tried before? If so, was it a success? If not, what prevented it? What is different now?
- Will any department feel threatened by this project?
- Is there any missing information?
- Are there any possible areas of confusion among stakeholders?
- What are the concerns that other managers might have about this project?
- What aspects of the project are the most sensitive to risk?
- Has anybody expressed concerns about the project?
- What is the appetite for risk at this time?
- How can project-related risk be mitigated?
- How strong is the risk section of the business case?
- What are the risks associated with a non-decision?

The risks faced by the buyer are internal, as well as external. They can be associated with issues of politics, history, culture and so on. For the seller focusing on the technical and even the business aspects of the buying decision these factors can be easily underestimated. A key question that the seller must ask is: 'Why has this not been done before?'

When there is an underlying risk sometimes it is easier for the buyer to make no decision at all. Hence, the buyer and seller must ensure the reason to act is sufficiently compelling as to overcome any inertia that may affect the decision. While all decisions entail risk, so too does a decision to do nothing.

We have talked a lot about buyer sensitivity to risk. However, it is important not to overplay the heightened levels of risk in today's more turbulent markets. For example, it can be tempting to assume that the present turbulent marketplace has hindered the ability or willingness of managers to make major decisions. This can be a dangerous and self-fulfilling prophecy that is not necessarily true.[i]

'Risk is something that the buyer has to be concerned with. Salespeople are remembered for their successes, while buyers are remembered for their failures. Buyers can have purchased millions, but will be remembered for the purchase decision and projects that went south. It is not surprising therefore that we are cautious.'

Buyer — Multinational Electronics Company

Risk And The Buying Process

Risk is another reason why helping the buyer follow their internal buying processes is essential. The buying process is an effective mechanism for managing risk as it:

- Ensures more thorough planning and analysis.
- Breaks the decision down into stages of incremental commitment.
- Brings the calculation of risk centre stage (often a business case section).
- Spreads responsibility for the decision over a wider group of mangers.

---

i   Just months after the threatened collapse of global economic order, some of the world's largest ever business deals were announced. This proves that some companies are responding to the new market environment with a new boldness. They recognise that a turbulent marketplace is the ideal arena for innovation and change.

Buyers commonly use price as a smokescreen for concerns surrounding unresolved risk. After all, it is easier to explain that 'the chosen supplier beat you on price', rather than 'we felt that we could not trust you.' That means tactics like dropping price, even if successful, are a costly way to address a fundamental buyer concern.

It is important for sellers to consider the full range of risk reduction strategies available to buyers including:

- Scoping projects and proof of concepts.
- Pilots and demos.
- Phased, staged, or staggered implementation.
- Iterative/agile implementation methodologies.
- New pricing models — pay per use, risk/reward and pay for performance.
- Risk management and contingency planning.
- Parallel systems/redundancy.
- Change management — people, process and systems.
- Project planning and review.
- Partnering with other trusted vendors.
- Joint planning and delivery with the buyer.

Building Buyer Trust

On paper you may clearly have the best product, technology or price. You may also have the best experts, the most impressive client list and the longest pedigree. However, all of these advantages will equate to nothing if the buyer cannot trust you or your team.

Firstly, the buyer has to trust the seller will deliver as promised and that the solution will meet its needs. But, perhaps more fundamentally, the buyer must trust the seller is looking out for their interests.

After all, projects may experience problems and unforeseen circumstances may arise, but knowing that the seller will steadfastly remain at the buyer's side, regardless of what happens, is arguably what matters most.

> **BUYER INSIGHT**
>
> 'We won't be working with that company,' the CTO of the buying organization said abruptly to the consultant retained to guide the purchase decision surrounding a new IT customer support system. 'I do not trust their account lead,' he added. 'There is just something that I don't like about him.'
>
> Suddenly, the lead contender, a global player whose team assumed it would be automatically in pole position for the contract, was sidestepped. The salesperson's calls were diverted to the consultant who made up some excuse for going cold on the supplier, one that did not require confronting the seller with the issues of trust.
>
> Life Insurance Company

Showing You Care

Inspiring buyer trust requires solid levels of competence, credibility and reliability. But most fundamentally it requires a demonstration that the seller cares. So, being an expert and having the answer is not enough to win trust.

The expert who is confident, perhaps overconfident, is at a disadvantage when it comes to building trust. The objective for the salesperson is not to show they know more, but that they care more.

Frequently we see salespeople trying to be best friends with a prospect and it backfires. It is only when you demonstrate to the buyer you genuinely care, trust is automatically built. The word genuine is important, because trust is difficult to fake.

Although it is only referenced directly in a limited number of places in this book, the principles of trust-based selling permeate all aspects of selling examined within this text.

The Trust-o-meter

What is your Seller Trustworthiness Index? Take the test – scoring each of the following statements as follows: 2 Always, 1 Sometimes, 0 Rarely):

☐ I have a record of putting customer interests first even when difficult to do.

☐ I genuinely care about customers and about making sure they succeed.

☐ I am candid about what I know and don't know.

☐ I am up front about what we can and cannot do.

☐ I am prepared to walk away unless a win-win is possible.

☐ I am willing to recommend a competitor, if in the prospect's best interest.

☐ I am fully transparent and honest in my dealings with customers.

☐ I really listen to customers' needs, thereby earning the right to give advice.

☐ I deal with unspoken issues, concerns and difficult issues.

☐ I show a personal interest in the buyer (e.g. personal interests).

☐ I always do what I say I will and I deliver on time.

☐ Even if the customer does not buy from me this time I stay in contact.

☐ I let customers see who I really am, rather than pretending to be someone else.

☐ I don't avoid the price issue and provide indicative price ranges if asked.

☐ I enable the customer to experience what I have to offer during the buying process.

☐ I spend very little time telling contacts how great my company is.

☐ I adopt a collaborative approach to working with clients — sharing work as it progresses, involving the customer in the process, working on site and keeping in touch at appropriate points in their process.

☐ I spend time with clients that might not be justified by a transaction-based qualification.

☐ I invest time in issues important to the customer even if only loosely linked to the sale.

☐ I invest in prospects that will not generate revenue this quarter or next.

Calculating your Seller Trustworthiness Score

31-40 points = Trusted (my word is my bond); 21-30 points = Trusted with a small 't' (I have conflicting loyalties and principles); under 20 = You like to take your chances!   Inspired by 'Trust-Based Selling' by Charles H. Green.

6. WALK IF YOU CAN'T TALK

There are some situations when the salesperson should cut their losses and bow out of preparing a proposal. The following are some important guidelines to help you decide when to bid and when to walk.

The Rise Of Competitive Tenders

Increasingly, it seems many buyers would rather read a sales proposal than see a salesperson. This is because the old way of interacting with salespeople has proved ineffective as far as the buyer is concerned. As a result salespeople are being kept at arm's length by means of the competitive tender or RFx (request for proposal, information and tender).

The growing popularity of the competitive bid means sellers are losing control over how they sell. In many cases they are being reduced to selling by email, fax and post.

> **BUYER INSIGHT**
>
> 'Vendors have to earn their stripes,' explained the purchasing manager in a major bank. 'A supplier may have to submit up to six responses for information (RFI), getting a polite "no" every time. What vendors need to realize is that we are not saying "no," as much as we are saying "not yet." We have thousands of suppliers we could do business with and sometimes the best way to find out exactly how and when is through the RFI process.'
>
> Procurement Manager, Tier 1 Bank

With the rise of competitive tenders, sellers are being forced to rely on a mixture of guesswork and prosaic writing. This is because instead of sending a well-trained salesperson, they are being forced to simply send a proposal.

Although it is an unreliable and unpredictable means of selling, difficult market conditions mean vendors may not have a choice but to comply.

To Propose Or Not To Propose?

In responding to competitive tenders the chances of winning, while unknown, are likely to be low. But even so, it takes courage to say no to a request for a competitive tender. However, sometimes this is the wise thing to do. Yet, many vendors automatically and instinctively respond to any request for a tender. Few companies have set criteria to determine when they will and will not tender. That means they are driven by how much they need or want a piece of work, as opposed to other considerations.

Are You Ready, Willing And Able?

Before putting pen to paper, make sure you are ready, willing and able to present a proposal to a new prospect. In public procurement we have been told that vendors need to do more to win. The advice from buyers is —

- Bid wholeheartedly or don't bid at all.
- Over deliver at each step of the defined buying process.
- Show conviction and passion.
- Show us the factors we are underestimating.

Before you prepare your next RFP ask yourself the questions shown overleaf.

A. Are You READY To Propose?

- Has there been sufficient interaction with the buyer?
- Do we have the information we need?
- Have we established sufficient rapport among the buying unit?
- Has there been sufficient access to and engagement with the buying group (including stakeholders) to ensure they own the solution?
- Have solution scope and budget parameters been tested or agreed?

B. Are You WILLING To Propose?

- Has the opportunity been reviewed internally?
- Is it business we want to go after?
- Are we prepared to invest the time?
- Will responding compromise other important sales activities?
- Do we believe we have a realistic chance of winning business now or in the future from this buyer?
- Has it been prequalified on budget, authority, timing and need?
- Is there an entrenched vendor?

C. Are You ABLE To Propose?

- Can we put together a good proposal in the time required?
- Do we have enough information?
- Do we fully understand the buyer's needs?
- Do we understand the essentials of the business case?
- Do we understand all the issues, constraints, nuances and risks?
- Do we have the solution they need?
- Do we have a relevant reference site/customer in their sector?

What Is Your RFx Budget?

Just like any other area of sales and marketing, RFx preparation should have a budget. Yet, few organizations set aside one and that is a mistake. It often means lax criteria regarding what tenders are, or are not to be completed. It also brings into focus the hit rate that is required in order to justify the investment that is made.

As one manager put, it 'Responding to requests for tenders that come in the post is a gamble, just like poker – if you don't decide what your limit is you could lose your shirt!'.

Setting Your Budget For RFx Preparation

The table below will help you to calculate what your organization spends or plans to spend on RFxs.

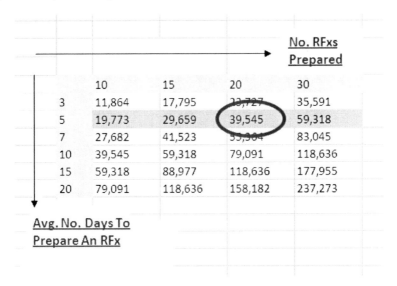

	No. RFxs Prepared			
	10	15	20	30
3	11,864	17,795	23,727	35,591
5	19,773	29,659	39,545	59,318
7	27,682	41,523	55,364	83,045
10	39,545	59,318	79,091	118,636
15	59,318	88,977	118,636	177,955
20	79,091	118,636	158,182	237,273

Avg. No. Days To
Prepare An RFx

Here is how it works:

- From the top row of the table, select the number of RFx responses to be prepared over a 12-month period. Then from the left-hand side select the average number of days required per RFx.
- For example, the figure circled in red $39,545 is the cost to prepare 20 (top row) RFxs, where on average five days (far left hand column) is required for each submission made.
- This is based on a calculation of the cost of that time based on a salary cost of $60,000, plus social insurance costs at 12% and expenses at 33% of salary.

When To Walk Away

Where the buying process is flawed or the relationship dysfunctional, a 'win-win' outcome for both parties is not going to be possible. Some examples include:

- Buyers expecting the seller to do all of the running. For example, they:
  - Ask for the submission of a proposal, while withholding important information and access to those involved.
  - Request unreasonably large upfront commitments of time and energy.
  - Expect an immediate solution to problems that may have existed for years.
- When **the level of respect for the salesperson** and, by extension, their company falls below that which is deemed acceptable.
- Where there is a **long-standing relationship with another vendor** or where work is traditionally undertaken in-house and this is deemed unlikely to change.
- The seller believes that **a compelling need or business case** does not exist.

The B2B Revolution Section 10

- The seller believes the **buying process is flawed** and the commitment is not evident on the buying side (e.g. senior managers are not involved) or prequalification criteria are not met.
- The project does not **meet internal criteria** regarding risk, profitability or other dimensions.

Increasingly managers frustrated with the time and energy sunk into futile RFx responses are setting down guidelines as to when they will participate. They are applying the simple rule — 'we will walk if we cannot talk.' That means unless the buyer is prepared to talk to the seller and to share sufficient information in advance of the RFx then a response will not be prepared. The result is those organizations are doing fewer, but better RFxs.

Applying Greater Science To The RFx

Many buying teams adopt a hands-off approach to vendors in a competitive tender process and many sellers have as a result started to treat RFxs very differently to other sales opportunities. That often means that, although competitive bids are more difficult to win, sellers are applying less science and sometimes less effort to them.

The sales team must apply as much as possible of their normal sales tool kit to the competitive tender. That includes principles such as:

- Nurturing the relationship in advance of any tender being published.
- Interacting with the buyer (within the constraints of the process) before submission and asking for the opportunity to interact once submissions have been received.
- Researching the buyer's industry and business drivers.
- Looking behind the needs set out in the proposal to identify implicit needs.

- Quantifying impact and modeling benefits.
- Augmenting the requirements of the buyer and innovating in terms of the solution.

'Yes, closed tenders create a level playing field, but we will be out for lunch with the buyer the week before the tender is published. We may even have helped to shape aspects of the tender. Just because it is a tender does not mean that the traditional aspects of selling and relationship building do not apply. It just means that they must be timed so as to precede going to tender.'

Operations Director — Global Systems Integrator

RFx Quality Checklist

In tandem with increased selectivity regarding what tenders will be submitted apply a quality improvement mindset. So, before you send your next response to a call for a competitive tender review it against the following checklist:

- Does it answer the requirements of the RFx and its key questions? ☐
- Does it demonstrate a unique understanding of their industry and its challenges? ☐
- Are customer references and other forms of third-party validation included? ☐
- Does it communicate business impact or results achieved? ☐
- Is the underlying business case addressed? ☐
- Does it clearly demonstrate your track record and credibility? ☐

- Are the key benefits of your solution clearly communicated? ☐
- Does it speak to the various stakeholders e.g. the CFO as well as the CTO? ☐
- Is it well presented and easy to read? ☐
- Does it display a thorough understanding of needs, including those that have been overlooked? ☐
- Does it explain you want to help the buyer decide and propose a low-risk next step? ☐
- Has it been carefully proofed by someone other than the author? ☐
- Has it been 'sense checked' by a senior manager before sending? ☐
- Does it meet your own internal risk prequalification rating? ☐

7. CLOSE AND NEGOTIATE WITH CARE

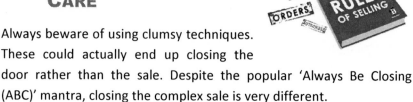

Always beware of using clumsy techniques. These could actually end up closing the door rather than the sale. Despite the popular 'Always Be Closing (ABC)' mantra, closing the complex sale is very different.

Closing techniques may work in the garage showroom or for door-to-door selling, but when it comes to the complex sale they hinder rather than help. In fact, by undermining trust, their effect is likely to be the opposite of what is intended.

Don't Rush The Buyer

The purchase is an important business decision, so the buyer won't be rushed into a premature decision. When everything is ready the buyer will know how to close and will readily do so. If the buying process has not been navigated successfully, no closing technique will close the sale.

In particular, looking for a yes on a proposal when there is a 'no', or 'maybe' in terms of the business case is futile. In these cases the seller must help the buyer make the business case more compelling if the project is to be approved.

As in all aspects of the complex sale the consultative approach works best. So, the question is not 'Are you ready to sign?' but 'What do you want to do next?'

Use the following questions to test if the sale is ready to be closed:

- How close to completion is the business case?
- How close to a decision do you think we are?
- Do you believe the business case is compelling?
- Do you have all the information you need?

- Do you think there is anything missing?
- Is there anybody else that you need to meet?
- Could there be any issues or concerns that remain unaddressed?
- What would you like to do next?
- Do the numbers stack up?
- Do you think the issues of the various stakeholders are adequately addressed?
- Do you think the time is right to go for executive/board sign-off?
- Are you confident in predicting the way they will decide?
- Is there anything you think could cause a decision to be delayed?
- Are there any events happening in the company that could impact on this?

Good Negotiation Cannot Compensate For Bad Selling

Just as we discussed with closing techniques, negotiating must be handled with care. It is not our intention to cover it in detail in this book – after all it could fill a book itself — however, we do want to share with you some cautionary advice on the subject.

The best advice as regards negotiation is not to do it until absolutely necessary. In particular, never mistake negotiation for selling. Salespeople who are drawn into negotiation before they have finished selling are in a no-win situation. After all, how can you negotiate before you fully understand what the buyer wants to achieve, what your solution should look like, the benefits to the buyer and your costs?

12 Reasons __Not__ To Negotiate:

Negotiating is not the solution in the following situations:

1. When you don't fully understand the buying process/decision and in particular what the buyer is trying to achieve.

2. When the sales task has not been completed, in particular before needs are clearly understood, alternatives have been explored and a solution defined.

3. When the business case has not been established and in particular the cost-benefit equation.

4. When it is too early in the sales cycle, in particular when there has not been sufficient interaction between buyer and seller.

5. When the needs of various stakeholders are not clearly understood or appear to be in conflict.

6. When the only issue on the table is price and when the value is not understood.

7. When project scope has not been tied down.

8. When there are unresolved or unspoken buyer concerns.

9. When your instinct tells you that something is 'not quite right'.

10. When the buyer's needs or priorities may have changed and you have not had the opportunity to fully understand the implications on the buying decision.

11. When you have not done your preparation and don't know the areas on which you can afford to concede tradeoffs.

12. When a genuine win-win is not possible, or you may not be able to live with the negotiated outcome.

THE ORDERS
REVOLUTION

'In order to provide salespeople with some extra ammunition in a difficult marketplace we gave them discretion with respect to discounts, as much as 20%. This was only to be used if necessary to clinch a deal.

After three months it became clear that the discount was being applied almost universally and put on the table as early as the third meeting with the buyer. The real problem was that when it came to the final negotiation the promised 20% had been long forgotten about and buyers wanted more. The lesson was clear, hold onto discounts until the very end.'

Sales Director — Industrial Equipment Manufacturer

Don't Play With Price

Always remember negotiation can't compensate for bad selling. This is particularly the case with respect to price. For example, if price is being discussed before the solution has been defined and its business impact established, then there is a more fundamental issue with respect to the progress of the sale and, indeed, the buying mentality.

Most negotiations take place on the basis of price. However, it is important for both buyer and seller to remember that price is only one of three core dimensions to the business case — costs, benefits and risk. The business case is a three-legged stool. If the two other legs of the stool – benefits and risk – are not up for discussion then things can easily topple over.

'As a professional buyer I know that I can get a 5% discount from the seller without any fuss. But, that is simply what has been built into the price from the start. To feel that I am really getting value I will need 10%, 15% or 20% and in the present climate that is a real possibility'.

Buyer — Financial Services Sector

There is certainly quite some mystique attached to the black art of negotiating. In particular it is often mistaken with influence, persuasion and even manipulation of another party to get what you want. To avoid this simplistic view the seller must focus on the buyer's business case. The negotiation must be characterized by transparency, integrity and a genuine search for the win-win.

Many negotiations involve a face-off situation where buyer and seller connive to get the upper hand. However, our experience tells us that all the negotiation techniques and ploys devised are useless unless there is a genuine focus on building a long-term partnership. After all, both parties are going to have to live with the negotiated outcome.

Don't Relax Until Everything Is Signed

The deal is not done until all the paperwork has been signed, the purchase order is in place and the first payment has been received. So remember even after the negotiation is over, never stop selling. There may be opportunities to add more value or add on extras as the buyer moves from closing the deal to worrying about its successful implementation and realizes the some aspects may have been overlooked. As one seller pointed out to us 'this is often the point at which you can win back the discounts that you had to concede in the sale by selling those items that the buyer had overlooked.'

8. WISH THEM WELL

When a vendor fails to win a sale after
issuing a proposal, regardless of a negative
outcome, the game is not over yet. There
are two important next steps required to

ensure that the investment in time, effort and resources does not go
to waste. Even if the buyer has chosen another vendor all is not lost.
You will live to bid another day. There will be future contracts and
there could even be problems with the chosen supplier.

You must remember the chances of the preferred supplier not
performing as expected are higher than you think. In fact, they could
be as high as one-in-four if buyer experiences with major vendors are
anything to go by (see Revolutionizing Repeat Sales). Some of these
vendors that disappoint will be replaced by the next in line and that
could be you. The chances of this happening are greatest at the early
stages of a project, for example where:

- The supplier runs into delivery problems.
- Reference calls on the supplier do not go as expected.
- Scoping work causes concerns for the buyer.
- Technical or proof-of-concept issues arise.
- Key early stage delivery dates are missed.
- The wrong project manager on the supplier side is appointed.
- A risk review committee raises a red flag regarding the projects
  viability.

It is important to be 'a good sport' in the face of rejection by the
buyer. Most importantly, genuinely wish the buyer well on their
chosen path and stay in touch as time elapses.

'We were very disappointed to learn that we had lost the deal to a competitor. I called the buyer to say best of luck and told him that if there was ever anything we could help with just call.

Two months later the call came. The chosen supplier had failed to deliver and the buyer wanted us to take over. We obviously had created a good impression during the sales process and by keeping in touch afterwards we showed our commitment and secured a phase one fee of €3 million.'

Sales Manager — IT Consulting Company

Five Tips On Wishing Them Well

1. Be genuine and sincere in wishing them well.

2. Don't in any way hint that they have not made the best decision (tempting though it may be!).

3. Make it personal — do it face-to-face or by phone.

4. Get everybody who has been involved in the sales effort to do it with their counterparts.

5. Keep in touch, sending useful information from time to time and expressing a genuine interest in how the project is proceeding.

Win-Loss Reviews

If you cannot be the supplier that wins, you can at least be among the select few to understand why a specific supplier won and learn from it. So, win-loss reviews are very important.

In most sales organizations win-loss reviews are sporadic and where they do take place they can be based on inadequate information regarding the real reasons for the buyer's decision. Furthermore, because they tend to point the finger at the salesperson, they can be subjective and struggle to deal with difficult truths.

Those organizations that effectively learn from the outcome of each sales bid, successful or otherwise, quickly outperform their less introspective counterparts.

Losing The Sale

All salespeople become emotionally involved in winning the sale. It is not just a financial issue involving commissions and targets, but also an issue of personal pride. With this in mind here are some tips on dealing with a lost sale:

- **Don't blame yourself, or anybody else**. Also, don't moan and complain either. Focus instead on what can be learned from the situation.
- **Don't personalize it**. If you feel you or somebody else dropped the ball, then focus your attention on the actions as opposed to the person. For example, it is not because John the account manager failed to close, but because the sales process employed fell short and needs improvement. Focusing on behaviors as opposed to people is key to transforming destructive criticism into positive direction.
- **Accept responsibility**. That is much different than accepting blame. Even if the market downturn, the departure of your contact in the prospect company and the actions of a competitor have played a role in losing the sale, it is best not to focus on these things, but instead on how you and your company deal with them. Accepting responsibility in this way is the key to leadership, to maintaining peace of mind and to moving forward.
- **Learn from it.** This offers the potential to transform a set back into an event that has the potential to improve your overall win

rate, or 'batting average'. So, ask yourself (and all the others involved):

- o What would your sales team do differently next time?
- o Did your team do everything it could do?
- o What worked well?

- **Undertake a win-loss analysis** in respect of every proposal or tender. That means asking questions such as:
  - o Why did it come as such a big surprise?
  - o What clues did we miss?
  - o What was the gap between our solution and the prospect's perceived needs?
  - o Did we fully understand the needs?
  - o Did we ensure the prospect had all the information required?
  - o Did we clearly build trust and establish credibility?
  - o Did we identify and address all the barriers?
  - o Could we have made it any easier to say yes?
  - o Did we invest enough time in building relationships?
  - o Did we cover the buying unit?
  - o Did we keep all our promises throughout?
  - o Were there any aspects of how we managed the sales cycle that could have been improved?

- **Ask for feedback and advice** from the prospect. Make it easy for the people involved to open up and tell you the real reasons. Take great care not to appear as a 'sore looser'.

- **Stay positive**. See the setback as an opportunity to grow, improve and become stronger. Remember, as Winston Churchill said, 'Success is moving from failure to failure without loss of enthusiasm.'

- **Revise the numbers**. Dealing with the implications head on is best. What is the worst-case scenario now that that potential sale is lost? How can you improve the situation, what will need to happen?

The Sales Orders Revolution — A Summary

The sales opportunity has been nurtured from the initial lead and the first meeting between buyer and seller. The lead that became a meeting that resulted in a sales cycle has progressed to the point of issuing a proposal to the buyer. That means that the seller is on the home straight, right? Well no — the risk of losing the deal is perhaps now at its greatest.

Getting the purchase sanctioned is going to take a lot more than the traditional sales proposal or closing technique. Indeed, those tools and techniques which sellers have traditionally relied upon to win the deal are no longer effective.

A radical overhaul of the sales proposal, negotiation and closing is required. That involves eight steps:

1. **Business case, before sales proposal.** The sales proposal, no matter how good it is, won't get a major purchase sanctioned. Only a compelling business case can do that. The implication is that sellers need to spend more time on the business case and less time on the proposal.

2. **Proposals, without surprises.** The only way to avoid surprises for both the buyer and seller is to ensure sufficient engagement prior to the preparation of any proposal. Proposals don't sell, or at least not very well. The golden rule is don't send a sales proposal when you should send a salesperson.

3. **Business impact, not benefits.** Benefits don't mean a lot to buyers. That is because they don't relate to those issues of interest to senior management. In short they don't quantify the impact buying the solution will have on the business.

4. **Write the last page first.** Sellers must write proposals the way buyers read them — that is starting with the numbers. Rather than sheepishly delivering a price, they need to communicate a credible and compelling return on investment.

5. **Think risk and insurance.** Risk is a part of the buying equation that sellers often overlook. That is because it often goes unspoken. However, to attempt to close or negotiate when there are outstanding issues of risk is likely to result in failure. Sellers need to create an environment of trust so risks can be brought out into the open and dealt with.

6. **Walk if you cannot talk.** There are some orders that you cannot win and in these cases it may make sense to cut your losses early. So having clear rules as to when you will and will not quote is vital. This is particularly important in the context of the rise of the RFx.

7. **Close and Negotiate with Care.** No aspect of selling is so dogged with misunderstanding than that of closing and negotiation. The result is the proliferation of out-dated closing and negotiation techniques that are completely at odds with the trust-based sale. Buyers are not falling for the phony 'good cop – bad cop' or the 'closing room only' close. These techniques are likely to close the door, not the sale.

8. **Wish them well.** It is important to avoid the appearance of being a 'sore loser'. It is surprising how many deals fall through in the early stages giving a second chance for the next in line. Maintaining a cordial relationship in spite of losing the deal can pay dividends.

These eight steps will enable the seller to carefully guide the opportunity through the often-tricky final steps of the sale. They bring to a successful conclusion all those efforts from the moment of inception of the lead, right through to the signing of the purchase order and have a fundamental impact on win rates. Then with the order signed it is time to start the process all over again, or is it?

Just as the salesperson thought that his job was done, a new equally, if not more, important chapter in the sale is about to begin. That is the delivery of the solution and the management of the customer relationship post sale. By doing this well the seller will be rewarded with repeat orders and referrals.

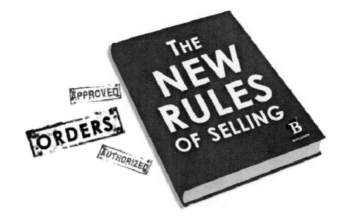

SALES
THE REPEAT
REVOLUTION

SECTION 11:
The Repeat Sales Revolution

THE NEW RULES FOR ACCOUNT MANAGEMENT

Developing Long-Term Relationships

Ensuring repeat sales and developing a long-term relationship with clients revolves around one simple but rarely completed equation — *Promise = Performance*.

While getting the first sale involves making promises, securing the second sale requires keeping them. Salespeople often feel they will lose a sale if they don't promise enough, but often lose out on subsequent sales by promising too much.

The ultimate measure of success for any organization is its ability to develop long-term customer relationships and repeat business. High rates of growth and profitability are unsustainable unless organizations can apply the same sophistication and skill to keeping existing customers as finding new ones. But the ability to nurture clients and grow existing business is one of the biggest failings of sellers, even though it requires half the salespeople, half the sales calls and half the proposals.

The equation *Promise = Performance* not only focuses organizations on delivering results and generating repeat sales, it also enables them to seek referrals from clients — one of the most effective ways to generate leads but also one of the most underutilized (a point we will cover later).

In order to meet a repeat sales target sellers need to redirect their efforts from helping the customer to buy, to helping the customer succeed. Thus, the role of a salesperson changes from making promises to keeping promises.

While this might sound easy, organizations are often complacent when it comes to their existing client base. Research highlights only one-quarter of promises made by vendors are being kept. This is good news for those taking on big name vendors, because as a result one-in-five managers are willing to consider changing from their existing supplier.

This section has been written to dispel the apathy that is traditionally associated with the topics of account management and customer service. It has been written to compel sellers to reposition repeat sales as the key success factor it truly is.

Delivering on Promises Made

Most companies are not allocating sufficient time and attention to managing and developing customer relationships. They are not applying the same level of structure and sophistication to the management of accounts as to other aspects of selling. Worse still, they are not delivering on all of the promises they make during the sales process. The result has been a revolving door approach to sales as companies win orders through selling, but lose customers through delivery.

A Change of Mindset

Vendors who reap the rewards of repeat sales view their relationship with existing clients in a far more enlightened way. The mindset change required is summarized in the table below:

	OLD Mindset	NEW Mindset
Role:	Supplier	Strategic Partner
Goal:	Winning The Sale	Winning The Customer
Strategy:	Closing The Next Deal	Helping The Customer Succeed
Approach:	Account Management	Account Development
Mindset:	Hunter	Farmer
Focus:	Winning New Business	Growing Existing Business

The New Rules of Account Management

Managing customer relationships to generate repeat sales requires the following shift in mindset:

1. Fire Half Your Sales Force.
2. Forget Customer Satisfaction.
3. Forget Customer Loyalty.
4. Forget Responding To Customer Needs.
5. Forget Account Management.
6. Forget Preferred Supplier.
7. Forget Up-Selling.
8. Forget Closing And Moving On.
9. Forget Marketing Yourself.

1. FIRE HALF YOUR SALES FORCE

Over the past decade companies developed an almost insatiable appetite for new customers. Meeting this need required more salespeople, campaigns and marketing. The irony is that most businesses would not have needed so many new customers if they could have kept more of those they had won.

A whole industry has developed to meet the challenge of finding new customers. As we have discussed it employs increasingly sophisticated sales techniques, expensive marketing campaigns and well-paid sales professionals.

However, the frenzied search for new customers results in a lot of waste. While organizations are winning orders, they are also losing customers. In times of buoyant demand this was not an issue, because replacing lost customers was easy. In today's market the reverse is true.

The disappointing reality is that many organizations are, relatively speaking, losing customers at the same rate as they are winning them. That means winning 20-25% of new prospects, while losing 20-25% of existing customers.

If organizations doubled the attention given to keeping customers, they could halve their sales force. While such a statement is meant to be provocative, it is also grounded in reality. Over the past decade most organizations we know would have celebrated on the achievement of a consistent growth rate of 10%, 15%, 20% per annum. However, many organizations typically lose at least twice that figure in terms of existing customers and revenue. That means a lot of selling time is being spent on finding customers to replace those who are leaving. Given the rising cost of the sale this is a reality that requires a real focus.

Split-Personality Selling

Sales and marketing has long suffered from a split personality. This is often described in terms of the hunter and farmer.

The hunter persona generally typifies the traditional view of the sales professional that aggressively seeks out customers in a proactive manner and rules supreme when there is buoyant growth in the economy. The farmer on the other hand is a more subordinate personality compared to the dominant hunter. The farmer's focus is on keeping and growing existing customers and is often undervalued within organizations. However, when times get tough farmers often become the savior of the sales department.

Most sales organizations are better at hunting than farming. This is generally because this has been where most emphasis has been placed. In the past it has not been a problem. Indeed, for the greater part of a decade 'hunters' have been celebrated, while their 'farmer' colleagues have often been berated for not generating enough new business.

With new customers now in scarce supply, the hunter often returns bloodied and empty handed. This is at a time when organizations are battling to maintain their existing client base as customer poaching reaches new levels. Those organizations that are great hunters, but poor farmers are struggling to meet their numbers.

'How many new customers should a salesperson be meeting every week?' was the first question the growth-hungry managing director asked the sales consultant. It was a loaded question. The director was clearly dissatisfied with the aggressiveness of the sales force in targeting new customers. In his own words, salespeople were doing more farming than hunting, spending too much time behind their desks and with existing customers.

The sales consultant suggested the answer would depend on the growth target and how it was split between new and existing customers, pipeline forecasts and average order values. He was happy to have resisted an immediate answer when an analysis of the company's sales pointed out that the average order value of existing customers was a lowly $8,000, with 56 of the company's 250 customers accounting for 90% of sales.

The company had a total of 10,000 accounts in its database across all its divisions. Clearly the problem was not one of hunting, but of farming. The company was more successful in winning customers than in keeping and growing them. How much time salespeople should be spending selling to new customers was a red herring. The real issue was, firstly, why the company had not succeeded in keeping past customers and, secondly, why they weren't selling more to existing customers.

Are You A Hunter Or Farmer?

The table below contrasts the 'hunter' versus the 'farmer' mindset. Circle the words in each column that most reflect your organization. Then compare the two columns to see where your organisation is to be found on the hunter-farmer continuum.

	HUNTER	FARMER
Account Mgt:	Reactive	Proactive
Motto:	'Close Them'	'Grow Them'
Role of Sales:	Sells and Moves On	Supports Delivery
Focus:	Short-Term	Long-Term
	Contract Value	Lifetime Customer Value
	Making Promises	Keeping Promises
Seen As:	Seller/Supplier	Strategic Partner/'Trusted Advisor'
Relationships:	Limited	Strong / At Senior Levels
Margins:	Average or Below	Above Average
Service:	Industry Average	World Class
Knowledge Of Customer:	Limited	Intimate

In an era when finding new customers is increasingly difficult and in turn more costly, the right mix of hunting and farming is essential. Ultimately, if your organization gets better at farming it could cut its sales force and still meet its targets! You get the point - a large amount of selling would be unnecessary if customers did not leave.

2. FORGET CUSTOMER SATSIFACTION

If customer satisfaction is how you are measuring your performance then prepare to be surprised. Traditional measures of customer satisfaction are a poor indicator of customer loyalty.

In our experience sellers typically overestimate the levels of loyalty and satisfaction of their customers. That is because they don't know what their customers are thinking and in many cases have failed to ask. Clumsy client feedback methods don't help either.

The result is that many suppliers have deluded notions regarding their importance to the buyer and the strength of the relationship. They think they are important when the buyer merely sees them as another supplier. Many sellers think they are safe, when in reality they are not.

> **SELLER INSIGHT**
>
> 'If the bar chart in the market research report puts customer satisfaction at 67%, the real score is somewhere between 47% and 57%. Most companies are really only scoring a 'C' on customer satisfaction.'
>
> Customer Loyalty Research Manager

Customer Satisfaction Is Meaningless

Satisfaction scores, often a source of pride for managers, can lead to complacency. This leaves suppliers vulnerable to client poaching from competitors.

Ticks on a questionnaire and pie charts in a report that relate to the satisfaction of a customer are likely to be neither accurate nor relevant. The bottom line is that relying on customer satisfaction as a measure of performance is deeply flawed.

There are a number of reasons why you should be wary of customer satisfaction survey results:

- The link between what customers tick on a questionnaire and what they do in practice is not a certain one. Responses to typical customer satisfaction questions are a particularly poor predicator of buying behavior or customer loyalty.
- Interpreting customer satisfaction results is not easy. You need to ask yourself just what is the real difference between a 6 out of 10 level of satisfaction versus an 8 out of 10?

The accuracy of the responses can be an issue. You have got to ask yourself:

- Will some of your customers inevitably 'hold back' to protect your sensitivities?
- Are you getting responses from the right people? Time and time again customer responses are provided by lower-level managers.
- How are you going to avoid the results being skewed? We find that customers who are either very satisfied or very dissatisfied are more likely to participate in customer satisfaction responses.

Depending on the methodology used in the survey and in particular the size and composition of the sample, the results are likely to be accurate at best to within +/- 3% of the actual result.

The lesson is simple — don't become complacent by relying on your customer satisfaction score.

Only One Measure Matters

The pursuit of customer satisfaction as the end goal of sales and marketing is misguided. Satisfaction is a fluffy and wooly concept that misses the whole point of the buyer-seller relationship. It is not the satisfaction of the buyer that matters, but the results you have helped them achieve.

Customer Satisfaction Surveys

Old measures:

How satisfied are you with the:

	Very Satisfied	Satisfied	Average	Dissatisfied	Very Dissatisfied
(a) Quality of service you receive	☐	☐	☐	☐	☐
(b) Quality of our solutions	☐	☐	☐	☐	☐
(c) Professionalism of our staff	☐	☐	☐	☐	☐
(d) Level of expertise provided	☐	☐	☐	☐	☐
(e) Speed of problem resolution	☐	☐	☐	☐	☐

New Measures:

a) What is the impact of our solutions on your business?
b) Are we improving your performance metrics?
c) How can we help you achieve your goals?
d) How can we better reflect your changing priorities?
e) What is the next challenge you are facing?

So, asking your clients if they are satisfied is simply the wrong question. It is time for sellers to get to the root of their relationships and ask what their impact is on their customer's business. This is more important than any other measure, such as customer satisfaction, loyalty or willingness to refer.

Sellers must measure themselves on the metrics used by their customers. So instead of saying 67% of our customers are satisfied or very satisfied, sellers should be able to say something like:

- 75% of our customers saved more than they expected using our solutions, with the average saving equating to 5% of total project costs.
- 1.25% was the improvement of margins resulting from the implementation of our solutions.
- Our customers have improved stock accuracy levels by 20% since the implementation of our solutions, with the net bottom line impact of 2%.

'Asking me if I am satisfied misses the point. I don't measure our suppliers in terms of satisfaction. I measure them on a five-point scale. This is part of our project review process, after all the performance of a project and a supplier is very closely intertwined.

OK, satisfaction has a role to play, but a nice warm feeling about a supplier does not get to the heart of how much a supplier is contributing to the achievement of our specific business objectives.'

Manager — Buyer UK Pharmaceutical Company

Sellers need to understand how their solutions are being used on a daily basis to fully understand the strength of their relationship with existing clients. They must also understand the impact on different tiers of the customer's organization — from managers to users and end customers. This of course is something that a customer survey cannot do.

The reality is that organizations are increasingly rigorous in evaluating vendors. Purchasing departments in some cases require that a vendor assessment is completed employing a standard template as follows:

Quarterly Vendor Evaluation Form

Criterion	Weight	Rating	Total
On Time Delivery			
Quality Levels			
Support Levels			
Responsiveness & Flexibility			
Communication			
Value for Money			
Commitment Shown			
Level of Innovation			
Level of Expertise			
Total Score			

Buyers tell us, however, they are rarely asked by suppliers about such evaluation procedures. That means suppliers are making assumptions about how they are being evaluated. Those buying organizations adopting best practice do strive to involve suppliers in the conduct of such reviews.

3. FORGET CUSTOMER LOYALTY

Sellers should ditch the old-fashioned notion of loyalty among customers. Loyalty is best left to football supporters and fan clubs.

When it comes to winning the next order sellers must expect buyers to make a cold and rational business decision regarding who can deliver the greatest value to their business. Sellers who assume otherwise are likely to be surprised. Now this is something that we have stated a number of times in this book, but it is something that is worth repeating.

The problem is that when it comes to repeat business many suppliers make the mistake of thinking they are safe when they are not. They assume that they are 'a shoe-in' for the next contract, but that belief is more often than not groundless.

Assuming you are 'a shoe in' puts you at a massive disadvantage, as the steps that would normally be applied to win the deal in a new sales cycle are often skipped.

Time For A Re-Think

To win the next order from an existing customer the seller must go back to square one. This is the only way they can ensure avoiding the danger of assuming they know what the customer wants or needs.

The seller must treat each repeat sale like a new sale. That means starting at the first step of understanding the customer's needs and requirements, talking to the various stakeholders, inputting to the business case and so on. It is important not to take any shortcuts or make any assumptions.

SELLER INSIGHT

'The renewal of the services contract was considered a sure thing and treated as booked revenue in the sales forecast. Our relationship with the customer spanned some three years. We had been through a lot together. As with any relationship there had been highs and lows, but overall we were confident that we had delivered and our relationship on the ground was strong.

We knew that competitors were sniffing around continually, but did not see this as a threat. We were aware that they would be asked to bid on the renewal but were assured by our sponsor that it was to be only a formality. When we were eventually told that the deal had gone to a competitor, we were amazed. We were blindsided by a change in strategy at the top of the organization, brought on by the arrival of two new senior managers. It taught us a valuable lesson — put the same effort into selling repeat contracts, as new ones.'

Medical Devices Manufacturer

4. FORGET RESPONDING TO NEEDS

Many organizations are in response mode when it comes to the needs of their customers. However, to keep pace with the accelerated rate of change in their customers' industries, a more proactive approach is required.

Most managers suggest they are 'not as proactive as they should be' when it comes to customer relationships. As a result they are often caught off guard when:

- A change in personnel in the customer's organization occurs.
- A new supplier appears.
- Negative customer feedback is received.
- Delivery or quality problems occur.
- Notice of contracts is put out to tender with no advance notice.
- Business priorities and strategies change that have a knock on affect on terms.

Be More Proactive

Sellers must be proactive, pre-empting customer needs and innovating constantly in terms of their solutions. That includes:

- Pre-empting problems the customer may have.
- Reviewing quality levels with the customer and how they can be improved.
- Looking beyond the scope of its project to the impact on other areas of the customer's business.
- Anticipating possible future needs of the customer.
- Sharing new ideas and opportunities for innovation or improvement.
- Holding follow-up reviews to understand how the solution is being used and how results can be maximized.

- Identifying how the total cost of its solutions can be minimized for the customer by eliminating or overhauling inefficient processes.
- Providing follow-up training courses to ensure widespread system adoption.

'Our project managers tend to get very focused on delivering the project, particularly the technical aspects. This often means they can lose sight of the bigger picture as regards the development of the relationship and future potential for work.

When the time comes around for account reviews we spend up-to 90% of the time discussing technical or logistical aspects of the project and fail to address the business and relationship dimensions adequately. Account reviews are rarely recorded in the CRM system so it is difficult to see what is done and what is not. If we don't get more proactive and structured in managing customer relationships we will miss our repeat sales target by 35% or more.'

Director — Professional Services Company

Moving Beyond Aspirations

It is clear that for many organizations there is a gap between aspiration and performance in respect of customer service.

The sad reality is that for many organizations, the terms customer retention, customer loyalty and customer satisfaction are mere buzzwords. They are not measured or managed, and do not get enough time and attention from sales, operations and the executive management team.

Forget About Marketing Slogans

It is clear that customer service requires more than vague aspirations or marketing slogans. Take for example companies who make bold promises about their commitment to customer service: 'High Performance Guaranteed', 'It's All About Customer Service'.

Ironically, however, independent vendor research at the height of the boom put customer disaffection at 25%+. Clearly customer service is more than a slogan.

Forget The Ad Hoc Approach

For far too many organizations the approach to customer relationship management is ad hoc, as opposed to structured and systematic.

The majority of companies (70%) from our benchmarking group are missing at least one of the basic ingredients of customer relationship management shown overleaf.

(a)   Sales And Profitability Analysis
      Classifying accounts based on revenue, profit performance and potential by employing activity-based accounting methods.

(b)   Client Feedback
      Gathering feedback from clients in a formal, systematic and documented manner.

(c)   Internal Reviews
      Bringing together the project team for each account to review performance, opportunities and actions.

(d)   Client-Side Reviews
      Undertaking reviews with clients at their premises to assess performance, identify any issues and understand changing priorities and directions.

(e)   Categorization Of Accounts
      Categorizing accounts with respect to performance and potential.

(f) **Policies/Targets**
Setting targets regarding service levels, responsiveness and performance for each different customer category.

(g) **Key Account Plans**
Developing a plan for each key account that sets out how to grow account revenue and profitability, as well as how to deepen the client relationship, and deliver greater value and service.

(h) **Revenue And Profitability Targets**
Setting and revising targets for revenue, as well as profits from existing customers and innovations in service/delivery to increase customer value.

(i) **CRM System**
Effectively employing a CRM system or sales database to store customer data and manage customer relationships.

> SELLER INSIGHT
>
> 'If organizations are not prepared to put the time and effort into the basics of account management then they don't deserve to keep their existing customers.'
>
> S
>
> Specialist Packaging Provider

5.   FORGET ACCOUNT MANAGEMENT

Customer accounts must be developed not just managed. Occasional internal account reviews and customer questionnaires are not enough to stop your competitors poaching your customers. Indeed, the best account management in the world won't be enough to keep and grow your existing customers.

If customers are viewed as no more than accounts, then the seller will be seen as no more than a supplier.

Indeed, the notion that suppliers can or indeed should manage their increasingly strong-willed and independent customers is absurd. The reality is that you cannot manage customers as you would manage a tax audit or class of unruly kids.

Another problem with the term account management is that it is too often seen as the role of one person, the account manager. However, strong customer relationships require the development of relationships between buyer and seller at all levels. While one person may be charged with overlooking the account, everybody from the CEO to the call centre representative has a role to play in that account's development.

Account management is something that needs to be ongoing and responsive, because the business environment each customer operates in is in constant change. Even though customer needs and priorities are unquestionably changing, many managers struggle to describe exactly how they are helping their customers respond to changing marketplace realities. As a result they are 'on the back foot' when faced by a demand for the re-negotiation of terms or a change in strategy.

Develop, Don't Manage

In a constantly changing marketplace, either a customer account is moving forward or it is moving backwards. That is not just in revenues, but in terms of the depth and strength of the relationship.

Unless you are continuously adding value, developing the relationship and, for example, innovating in terms of delivery, then your client is vulnerable to being poached by a competitor.

From the customer's perspective it is your organization's performance last week and last month, not last year or the year before, that matters.

Suppliers cannot live long on their laurels, hence the importance of ongoing innovation and improvement. To be secure, the supplier must anticipate their customer's present and future needs and engage in an ongoing dialogue about these needs.

Focus On Client Success

The main difference between account management and account development is the focus on client success. So, the right question is not 'how are we managing the account?' but 'how are we helping the customer to succeed?'

Let's be clear about the real difference between account management and account development, as shown in the table below.

Account Managent Vs Account Development

	OLD: ACCOUNT MANAGEMENT	NEW: ACCOUNT DEVELOPMENT
Mode:	• Reactive	• Proactive
Focus:	• Transaction	• Relationship
	• Short-term	• Long-term
Relationship:	• Supplier	• Strategic Partner or Trusted Advisor
Key Measure:	• Customer Satisfaction & Loyalty	• Customer Success or Results
Objective:	• To Sell More	• To Help More
Responsibility:	• Account Manager	• Everybody
Customer Knowledge:	• Limited	• Intimate

Account development is a long-term proposition and views relationships as more than the sum of individual contracts or projects. It is where the seller believes 'we can be good together' and demonstrates to the buyer that they want to contribute further to their success. In respect of key accounts the supplier strives to be more than just a supplier — their aim is to become a strategic partner.

In order to make good on this promise the seller needs to understand the evolving dynamics of the buyer's business and connect with the buyer's strategic objectives. The seller has to invest in building the relationship post sale, seeking to ensure their contact base is higher, wider and deeper within the customer's organization.

Innovation is one of the most important characteristics of this special type of relationship and is reflected in the two-way exchange of ideas between supplier and customer.

6. FORGET ABOUT CUSTOMER EQUALITY

Loyalty works both ways and the vendor must determine which customers it will commit to for the long term.

Therefore those sellers committed to growing repeat business have by necessity to dispense with the notion 'all customers are equal.' They need to segment their customers according to their needs and more importantly their strategic importance.

The reality is that serving customers does not just drive revenues; it also drives costs. Therefore sellers must focus any investment in this area on those customers that are most deserving. That means the most demanding customers are not necessarily first in line for greater attention, service and support, but those that offer the greatest long-term potential.

Sellers will inevitably outgrow certain customers, such as those that are less profitable. They must focus on those that represent the best strategic fit for their business and afford the greater potential for long-term growth. However, it is the customer's view of any such strategic fit that is vitally important and will ultimately determine the nature of the relationship.

7. FORGET BEING A PREFERRED SUPPLIER

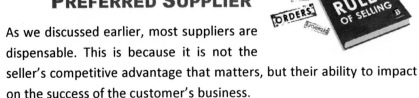

As we discussed earlier, most suppliers are dispensable. This is because it is not the seller's competitive advantage that matters, but their ability to impact on the success of the customer's business.

The seller's ultimate goal in respect of key accounts is to become so important to the customer as to become embedded as a strategic partner. That means reaching a new level of interdependence and synergism that effectively makes the supplier's position unassailable. The result is a two-way partnership for success.

From Supplier To Strategic Partner

The path from supplier to strategic partner is a long road on which many set out, but few ever truly arrive. It is also a journey that requires extraordinary effort and commitment over a long period of time. This fact explains why we often overestimate the true progress of the relationships we have developed with customers (as illustrated in the following diagram).

Supplier ─X─ · ─ · ─X· ─→ **Strategic Partner**

You think you are here

This is where you really are!

The supplier must demonstrate not only its capability to deliver, but a genuine commitment to the buyer's success. Key elements of building such a strategic relationship are when:

- The supplier contributes to the achievement of an important customer objective or strategy in a manner that is visible, quantifiable and direct.
- The supplier has access to the buyer's boardroom and is considered a trusted advisor.
- The customer calls on the supplier's expertise.
- The supplier's products and skills are considered to be specific or at least tailored to the unique requirements of the customer and its industry.
- The seller goes beyond meeting the customer's present needs by anticipating future needs.
- The seller goes beyond merely providing products and services to the client, and focuses its resources on impacting on the customer's business.
- The seller 'blurs the lines' between the customer and supplier relationship by:
  - Sharing people, ideas, technologies and so on.
  - Inspiring the buyer, through innovation and leadership.
  - Involving customers in product/process development.
  - Integrating processes, systems, supply chains and shared assets.
  - Sharing the risk and the reward, including new commercial models.

S

It was the first time the CTO had received a call from a chairman of one of the company's suppliers. Introducing himself as the chairman and non-executive director of the company's prime contactor on a major new systems project, he explained that the company's project had been reviewed at a high-level at the most recent board meeting — something that is standard policy for key projects. 'It is a very interesting project and one that we are really excited about. I understand we are a little ahead of schedule at this time and intend to stay that way as the project progresses', he added.

'I know this is a very important project for you and I just wanted to say that you can at any time call myself or the CEO directly if you would like to discuss any aspect of the project. Your account manager knows this and he won't in any way be put out as we will be working together to support him in making this project a real success.'

The CTO did not have much to say in reply, other than "Thanks". As he hung up the phone he was even more convinced that the supplier would deliver.

CTO UK Retail Bank

8. COMMITMENT TO THEIR SUCCESS

Getting the first sale requires helping the customer to buy. However, ensuring you get the second sale will come down to your ability to ensure your customer's project succeeds.

Do your customers see your company as being genuinely and passionately committed to their success? The answer to this question is perhaps the ultimate measure of your company's ability to sell more to its existing customers.

Growing revenue from existing customers requires identifying not just opportunities to up sell and cross sell, but new ways to contribute to the client's short, medium and long-term success.

BUYER INSIGHT

B 'Projects go awry and often for reasons outside the control of the vendor. Indeed, the bigger and more complex the project, the greater the risk that there will be setbacks and surprises. We have been around for long enough to know that. We are quite realistic in our view of the world and in particular how we measure the performance of suppliers. In this respect the supplier who faces setbacks on a project, but recovers from them well can impress us more than the supplier for whom a project is plain sailing. The problems may not even be the responsibility of the vendor; it may be a hold up on our side. The vendor that rows in behind us to solve the problem will be remembered.'

Program Manager — Financial Institution

Focus On Sharing Success

While organizations can rely on their commission-led sales teams to seek to capture a greater share of the customer's total possible spend, they can readily overlook opportunities to contribute more tangibly to the customer's success.

Sales managers often ask 'how can we take more revenue from that account?' However, suppliers need to change the focus from 'how can we take more revenue from that account' to 'how can we help the customer more?'

Key Account Review Questions

To sell more you need to revitalize the questions you ask before engaging in internal or client-side account reviews. Think like the customer.

OLD QUESTIONS	NEW QUESTIONS
How can we:	How can we help the customer:
Sell more to them?	Achieve more?
Get them to buy more from us?	Achieve more for less?
Take more from that account?	Cut costs?
Identify follow-on sales opportunities?	Minimize risk?
Up-sell and cross-sell?	Do more in-house?
Increase our share of the customer's category spend?	Address key priorities?
Dislodge another supplier?	Shift costs from cap-ex to op-ex if appropriate?
Tie the buyer in for a longer term?	Stage costs?
Sell to other parts of the business?	Stretch their budget?
Maximize margins?	Look good?
	Accelerate results/progress?
	Avoid over-runs?

SELLER INSIGHT

Most account reviews focus too much on the salesperson's perspective. They are typically narcissistic account reviews. It is all about — Me! Me! Me! The focus is on how to sell more rather than how to help the client succeed more.

Throughout the entire review, there is typically no mention of the buyer's:

- Changing priorities
- Satisfaction
- Needs and unmet needs
- Expectations and perceptions
- Problems and challenges
- Opportunities
- Anxieties and concerns
- Metrics

If an account review does not look to help the buyer more and in return sell more, then it is starting from the wrong place.

Sales Effectiveness Coach

Help Customers Meet Their Target

To meet your target then you must help the customer meet their target too. So, rather than looking to take an even larger share of the buyer's limited budget, sellers must look for new ways to:

- Make the buyer's budget go further.
- Help the buyer do more for less.
- Accelerate the buyer's progress towards their goals.

There must be a visible link between the supplier's solutions and the customer's success. However, suppliers cannot assume that customers fully appreciate the value they are adding or impact they are having. So, it is the supplier's job to make sure this is very clear.

As customer success is the goal of the salesperson and business impact is the measure of that success, then the formula by which it will be measured and the process by which it is to be documented are vital. In short, the job of the sales and delivery organization is to document and discuss success right throughout the customer relationship. To sell more, you need to reinforce success more.

9. FORGET CLOSING AND MOVING ON

'Close them and move on' has been the modus operandi of selling for too long.

However, just as the salesperson thinks their job is done, another vital phase of the sales process is just about to begin — implementation.

If the salesperson moves their entire focus onto winning new business, who will ensure that:

- The promises made are kept?
- The delivery is successfully project managed?
- The various stakeholders are satisfied?
- The relationship is nurtured and developed?
- The contribution to the customer's success is clearly demonstrated?
- The next sales opportunity is identified?

Can the salesperson trust those in account management and delivery to make good on all the promises that have been made?

Keep Promises, Deliver Results

As many as four out of ten promises made by vendors are not being kept, according to buyer feedback in respect of some of the world's largest sellers. This astonishing fact comes from the work of the highly reputable research organizations, including CSO Insights.

Vendors are constantly undermining the success of their business by tripping up over their own unfulfilled promises. They constantly make promises in sales meetings, sales presentations and sales proposals but neglect to deliver.

Keeping promises can be tricky. Indeed, if the road to the first sale was complex and bumpy, then the way to the next one is likely to be even bumpier. That is because once the sale is closed, the real work of implementation and delivery begins. To paraphrase Winston Churchill — The sale is not the end; it is not even the beginning of the end. It is simply the beginning of the beginning.

The complex sale involves complex delivery. Issues involving multiple stakeholders, complicating factors, risks and constraints that marked the sale, will also be manifest in the delivery. This is often complicated further by things changing during the time lag between the signing of the agreed proposal to the actual start of a project.

Regardless, most major projects require a significant element of change management, as newly formed teams and relationships find their own level, and people and processes come to grips with the new technologies and solutions.

Planning Major Projects

Analysts suggest that as many as four out of five IT projects are over budget, behind schedule or otherwise struggling. The statistics underline the fact that the challenges involved in successfully delivering a project are as great as those involved in winning the order in the first instance.

Get Off To A Good Start

Evidence highlights the early stages of a project always have an inordinate bearing on overall project success. That is because:

- The project planning stage can be risky for both supplier and customer.
- Initial confidence can dip as users come to terms with change.
- The original sales team and senior buying team are replaced by project managers, account managers and delivery teams that have their own views and experiences.
- Early wins are important in galvanizing support for any project.

So it makes sense that the lead sales people handhold and support the customer at the early stages of a project.

The *Guardian* newspaper reported in 2009 that the UK's largest non-military computer project, a £13 billion NHS (National Health Service) project, ran aground. Two of the contractors, Accenture and Fujitsu, quit while BT announced a multi-million write down on the project. Incidentally, this is something BT had to do against 15 of its biggest 17 contracts, according to the paper.

This story is further evidence that the way IT is bought, sold and delivered, like so many IT projects themselves, is broken. Fixing it is both an opportunity and a challenge facing sales professionals in the industry.

The savvy seller must deal head on with very real project risks around delivery and cost. The salesperson's job description has changed from selling, to helping prospects regain confidence and maximizing the chances of project success.

Passing The Baton

With lengthening sales cycles, the salesperson is likely to be under pressure once the deal has been signed to move on to close the next opportunity. However, the danger is that those involved in the negotiation have moved on at a time when buyer anticipation and anxiety is at its greatest.

Buyers often complain the attention, enthusiasm and commitment shown by sellers during the sales process wanes once the order is signed. Instead of the seller chasing the buyer, the situation can be quickly reversed. This happens all too often when the salesperson fails to successfully pass the baton to their colleagues.

The salesperson should never shirk the responsibility of ensuring project success. However, it is essential that they hand over the day-to-day project management and delivery to the experts. Buyer confidence depends on a smooth transition, so it is crucial that the person who takes over the day-to-day management of the project has been involved during the sales process. It is also really important for the salesperson to maintain contact with their delivery team and the buyer's implementation team. Salespeople cement and deepen the relationship by staying in touch throughout the lifecycle of a project.

Delivering On The Business Case

Vendors need to take greater care to keep promises and deliver the expected results. That is the golden rule of success and it remains unchanged with time. The vital equation is not just *promise = performance*, but *performance = results*.

BUYER INSIGHT

'For our business the key elements of change **B** management are as important as the technology. That includes process re-engineering, as well as user training and support. All of this sounds obvious, but it has had profound implications in terms of how we organize our business. In particular, it has transformed our view of project and vendor success.'

CTO Insurance Company

10 Common Mistakes In Project Delivery

These 10 mistakes have a major impact on a salesperson's ability to win repeat business:

1. Loss of scope (parameters not tied down in negotiation).

2. Poor management of expectations.

3. False starts and poor handovers.

4. Failing to deliver early wins.

5. Poor change management processes.

6. Failure to get ownership and buy-in.

7. Loss of time trying to make inefficient processes better.

8. An over emphasis on a speedy implementation.

9. Failure to track progress and communicate results from day one of the project.

10. Failure to manage the project's financial performance.

BUYER INSIGHT

'The functionality of our products had become such that only a handful of users were exploiting their capability to the full. To use an analogy our solution had developed into a Ferrari, while most users were only driving it like a mini. Clearly our sales task was not complete when the order was won. We had to find a way to support our users in exploiting the full potential of our solutions within their businesses. We made a major investment in user training, accreditation and support, in particular in eLearning. This has created a new revenue stream for our business, while also locking in our customers to our products for the long-term based on realizing the potential to impact on their business.'

Financial Services Company

10. FORGET MARKETING YOURSELF

At a time when most marketing goes straight into the buyer's bin, many sellers are overlooking the cheapest and most powerful of all marketing — customer references and case studies. In a sample of companies we reviewed only 50% were actively using testimonials in their marketing, while only 40% were actively seeking customer referrals or introductions.

Your Most Powerful Marketing

The people who can best market your solutions are not on your payroll and they never will be. Yet, they can:

- Grab the attention of your customers better than any press release.
- Communicate more effectively than any brochure.
- Convince better than any salesperson.

These same people speak your customer's language and know exactly the issues that concern them most. These people are your customers.

Vendors have been trying to tell buyers how great their solutions are, but they are not listening. They are only interested when they hear it from their peers. They want to hear from customers, not supplier marketing departments.

The reality is that if you do a good job at ensuring your customers' success, you can almost forget about marketing yourself. Your customers will do your marketing for you.

Enlisting Your Customers

So, how can you get your customers to do your marketing for you? Well, firstly you need to have demonstrated a genuine commitment to the client's success. If you help boost the client's success you can be confident they will be glad to repay you by telling others of your work.

Customers can contribute to your marketing along a progressive scale in terms of impact and commitment, as follows:

7 Ways Customers Can Contribute to Your Marketing

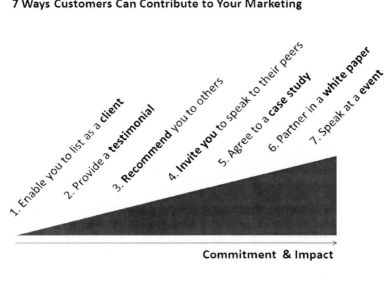

Commitment & Impact

This list is not exhaustive, but it does show a deepening commitment on the part of the buyer to helping the supplier's business succeed. Getting written testimonials from customers is powerful. However, the real power of the customer as marketer comes when they are driven by a desire to promote their own achievements and refer you to their peers.

SELLER INSIGHT

S

'We set about writing some case studies about the successes we have achieved with our customers. In particular we wanted people to know that our most recent pharmaceutical client had cut waste output and associated costs by 25% thanks to our services.

Our marketing team decided to go one step further. Not content to write case studies from our perspective they wanted to facilitate the customer in publicizing its own success. They arranged a number of trade magazine interviews and a speaking slot for the company at an industry event. The seller talked mostly about its success, we didn't get our glossy case study but we did get really strong reference material out in the public domain. The fact that the customer was promoting himself made the impact all the more powerful.'

Environmental Services Company

The Power Of Referral

All too often referrals and recommendations — the most powerful form of sales lead possible — are left to chance with less than 40% of sales people we deal with actively seeking customer referrals or recommendations to sell to others. How many of your customers have been asked for a referral in the past year?

It is important to set a target for the number of referrals you need to get over a 12-month period. Indeed, the closure rate from customer referrals is likely to be two or three times that of normal sales leads. In addition to higher win rates, referrals can result in faster buying cycles. When you are introduced or referred, you are marked aside from the traditional salesperson; you gain a badge of trust and credibility that can move you to the inner circle and ensure you are treated as an expert and problem solver.

'A growing number of our clients have realized that the information provided by traditional questions such as "On a scale of 1 to 10, how would you rate your level of satisfaction with our company?" is not very useful in predicting customer behavior.

As a result they have adopted "willingness to refer or recommend" as a proxy for customer loyalty and satisfaction. It is called the Net Promoter Score.'

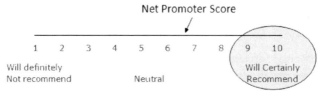

Q. On a scale of 1 to 10 how willing would you be to recommend our company to a colleague or friend?

Net Promoter Score

1 2 3 4 5 6 7 8 9 10

Will definitely Not recommend   Neutral   Will Certainly Recommend

A Net Promoter Score (NPS) metric — based on the methodology of Fred Reichheld, Bain & Company and Satmetrix — is a more accurate customer behavior indicator. These measures are measured quarterly and inputted directly to the performance reviews and bonuses of client-facing staff in a growing number of sales organizations.

International Research Manager

The Repeat Sales Revolution — Summary

All of sales and marketing is obsessed with winning the next customer. Meanwhile, many businesses are hemorrhaging as many as one-in-four customers annually.

The simple message of delivering on promises and keeping existing customers is a familiar one for most managers, yet issues of customer service and satisfaction receive only lip service. Organizations need to tackle the apathy and complacency that surrounds their relationship with their existing base of clients.

The new rules of repeat sales are as follows:

1. **Fire half your sales force.** The sad reality is that if companies got better at keeping their existing customers they could meet their growth targets with much fewer salespeople. If they applied the same sophistication to keeping customers as to winning new ones they would be much better off.

2. **Forget customer satisfaction.** Marketing slogans love to talk about the importance of customer service and customer satisfaction, however it is only a red herring. Buyers have moved beyond satisfaction as the basis for selecting suppliers — they want suppliers that impact in a tangible way on the performance of their business.

3. **Forget responding to customer needs.** Too many suppliers are playing catch-up in terms of changing customer needs and priorities. They are waiting for customers to tell them what they want, while competing suppliers are tempting them with innovative solutions, ideas and technologies.

4. **Forget account management.** Account management is crawling rather than running in many companies, with basic elements, such as key account reviews and plans, severely lacking. Yet, remedying the deficiencies in account management is not going to be enough. Sellers need to develop, not just manage their accounts.

5. **Forget preferred supplier status.** Suppliers are a dime a dozen in today's competitive market space. The real test is to become so important to the customer as to be indispensable. That means to transition from supplier to strategic partner.

6. **Forget up-selling.** Naturally, account reviews focus on selling more to the customer, however they neglect the basis upon which the next sale is predicated. That is the commitment of the supplier to meeting the customer's needs. To meet sales targets suppliers need to show their customers how they can help them meet their own targets.

7. **Forget closing and moving on.** Longer sales cycles mean that once the deal is closed the seller is under increasing pressure to find and close the next deal. However, the seller must stay involved post sale in order to ensure success.

8. **Forget marketing yourself.** A testimonial or referral from a customer is worth dozens of adds, cold calls and marketing brochures. Yet, this powerful form of marketing is often overlooked by vendors.

The B2B Revolution Section 11

SECTION 12:

Conclusion

CALL TO ARMS – CALL TO ACTION

A Quick Recap On The Revolution

In Part 1 we witnessed first-hand how buying has changed – a revolution in the people, processes and logic of today's buying decisions. The implications for selling are profound.

As discussed in Part 2 once successful sales techniques and campaigns are now failing to deliver. The reality is that last year's cold calls, meetings and proposals are increasingly missing the mark.

Fig. 12.1: The Implications Of The Buying Revolution in Summary

The following aspects of buying **have** been transformed:	That means those sellers who have **not** adapted are:
Buying Process	Selling the wrong way
Business Case	Selling the wrong thing
Buying Team	Selling to the wrong people

As the table above suggests there are implications for the salesperson, the sales process and the sales proposition. In short The Buying Revolution™ requires a revolution in selling. That is a revolution at each stage of the sales process – from leads to orders and all steps in between.

There are 41 new rules of selling and one new over-arching role – that is to help the buyer to buy. These form the new basis of competition in selling. They present great opportunities as well as great challenges for every seller.

Some Words Of Encouragement

With the bulk of the book now completed, it is time for a motivational – 'Yes we can!' Let's start by recognizing that the contents of this book, while radical and revolutionary, are well within your grasp.

We have seen many businesspeople, as well as salespeople from all backgrounds, apply these principles and achieve a major boost in their success rates as a result. Yes, they were challenged by many aspects of what today's buyers want – they even found some of the changes quite uncomfortable at first. However they consistently tell us that the challenges involved were greatly out-weighted by the opportunities.

A Message Of Great Optimism

It is with confidence therefore that we can state that 'those sellers who adapt to the changed nature of organizational buying will enjoy a significant boost to their success'.

As you will recall from the introduction, we estimate that boost at 33% – a figure based on a modest 3% improvement in the level of activity and effectiveness at each stage of the sales process (i.e. leads, meetings, cycles, orders and repeat sales). By taking action based on what you have read this advantage can now be yours.

Time to Take Action

Buyers have spoken and by reading this book you have listened. Now it is up to you what you do about it.

- Will you act on what they have told you?
- Will you adjust how you sell to how your customers buy?
- Will you make the transition from selling to helping the buyer to buy?
- Will you make the giant leap from seller to trusted advisor?
- Will you overhaul your sales process?

Our job has been to publish the new rules of buying, to prevent other salespeople having to second guess what buyers want or what sales techniques they should or should not use. With this information you can revolutionize your sales and thereby steal business away from those sellers unable, or unwilling to change.

Revolutions Create New Possibilities

Revolutions take from some and give to others. They upset the old world order, deposing old competitors, channels and markets, while creating new ones in their place. They create winners as well as losers. The difference between the two is the application of the principles in this book.

Let us be clear about it, *The Buying Revolution*™ will result in casualties — but neither you, nor your team need be among them. Specifically, it threatens to overthrow and depose those sellers who are unable or unwilling to change. Perhaps they don't realize that change is needed or just exactly what changes to make.

It is Time For a Transformation

Revolutions entail a major leap from the old to the new — new methods, technologies and viewpoints. In respect of The Buying Revolution™ the following are among the most fundamental of those 'out with the old and in with the new' transformations required:

The Top 5 Transformations Required by The Buying Revolution™

Out with the OLD:	In with the NEW:
Salesperson	Trusted Advisor
Selling	Helping The Buyer To Buy
Sales Proposal	Business Case
Sales Process	Buying Process
Buying Decision	Business Decision

Planning Your Personal Revolution

The table shown above is merely a summary of a checklist to be found in Appendix A. So, we recommend that is where you go next. It is a useful tool that summarises this book on four pages and will enable you to track your very own professional sales revolution on 4 levels:

I. Who You Are

III. How You Think

II. What You Do

IV. The Results You Get

We call it The Revolution-o-meter – a tool, or checklist to enable you to take the temperature of, or gauge your response to The Buying Revolution™.

In Appendix A you will find a tool, or checklist to gauge your selling and specifically the extent to which you are applying the principles of The Buying Revolution".

THE SELLING
REVOLUTION-O-METER
^

The Revolution-o-Meter

Use the Revolution-o-meter to pinpoint where you are on the journey from old to new as shown in the excerpt from Appendix A shown below.

I. WHO <u>YOU</u> ARE: Your Professional Revolution

On a personal-professional level how have you adapted to the increased sophistication of your customers and their buying processes? Mark your progress on the journey from left (pre-revolution or out of date) to right (post revolution, or ideal).

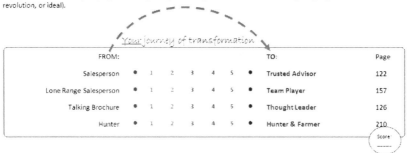

FROM:							TO:	Page
Salesperson	•	1	2	3	4	5 •	Trusted Advisor	122
Lone Range Salesperson	•	1	2	3	4	5 •	Team Player	157
Talking Brochure	•	1	2	3	4	5 •	Thought Leader	126
Hunter	•	1	2	3	4	5 •	Hunter & Farmer	210

Score
_____

On the left-hand side above is the legacy of selling, which we have all inherited but must now reject. On the right-hand side is the future of selling, which we must embrace. We must steadfastly make the journey from left to right.

Each of us will make the transformation at our own pace, but for all of us there will be many challenges along the way. With this in mind we have referenced the page number that is relevant to each of the changes required in the far right hand column of the tool in Appendix A.

Some Final Tips

To conclude here are some final tips on applying the contents of this book to your success:

- The principles and techniques presented in this book will boost your results, but like everything else the benefits will only come after as **sustained effort** has been put in. One thing for sure is that it is not a quick fix. Given the long sales cycles involved in the complex sale the results will take time to translate into sales commission.

- **Deconstruct your sales process** along the lines presented in Part 2 – that is examining the specific opportunities and challenges in respect of each stage from leads to orders and all steps in between. Each area presents its own opportunities and challenges

- It will take a determined effort over a long period of time and it requires a **consistent, integrated approach** across all aspects of your sales process and across all of the 41 new rules for lead generation, sales meetings, and so on as presented in Part 2 of this book. Implementing just one of the changes recommended by buyers in this book won't be enough.

- One approach is to **adopt one chapter at a time**, one idea at a time. After all a journey of a thousand miles begins with a single step, so take one step today and another tomorrow. Start with those ideas and techniques that you feel most comfortable with, go for the early wins so to speak.

- Use the book as a daily resource, as **a manual in your day-to-day activities**. Share it with your colleagues and use it to revolutionize selling organization-wide, after all if you adopt the principles and your colleagues do not then your good efforts could easily be undone.

- You will find **lots more tips, insights** and encouragement online at www.theBuyingRevolution.com and if you would like our help you will also find our contact details there.

Viva la revolution!

APPENDIX A:

The Revolution-o-Meter

MEASURING YOUR RATE OF CHANGE

The Buying Revolution™ requires fundamental changes by salespeople on four levels:

I. Who You Are   III. How You Think

II. What You Do   IV. The Results You Get

That is a series of 'from - to' transformations from left to right in each of the following pages. Use the rating scales to mark where you are presently located on each dimension. Total up each page and when you have completed the exercise you can calculate your overall rate of progress by reference to the instructions at the end.

I. WHO <u>YOU</u> ARE: Your Professional Revolution

On a personal-professional level how have you adapted to the increased sophistication of your customers and their buying processes? Mark your progress on the journey from left (pre-revolution or out-of-date) to right (post revolution, or ideal).

Your journey of transformation

FROM:	*Circle your present rating:*					TO:	Page
Salesperson	●	1	2	3	4	5 ●	Trusted Advisor	200
Lone Ranger Salesperson	●	1	2	3	4	5 ●	Team Player	232
Talking Brochure	●	1	2	3	4	5 ●	Thought Leader	138
Hunter	●	1	2	3	4	5 ●	Hunter & Farmer	296

Score: _____

II. WHAT YOU DO: Your Behavioral Revolution

How has your daily sales approach, or behavior responded to The Buying Revolution™? Circle the scale below to show your position on the scale from left (pre-revolution or out-of-date) to right (post revolution or ideal).

FROM: OLD BEHAVIOR		Circle your present rating:					TO: NEW BEHAVIOR	Page
Find Demand	●	1	2	3	4	5 ●	Creates Demand	138
Generate Leads	●	1	2	3	4	5 ●	Nurtures Contacts	124
Seek To Control (The Buyer)	●	1	2	3	4	5 ●	Seeks To Coach (The Buyer)	28
Rely On Slick Sales Techniques	●	1	2	3	4	5 ●	Shun Slick Techniques	195
Sell Low (mid & low level managers)	●	1	2	3	4	5 ●	Sell Higher & Wider	58
Sell, Sell, Sell	●	1	2	3	4	5 ●	Help Buyers To Buy	28
Write Sales Proposals	●	1	2	3	4	5 ●	Influence the Business Case	240
Study Selling (books, courses, etc.)	●	1	2	3	4	5 ●	Study Buying (books, courses, etc.)	73

Score: _____

III. HOW YOU THINK: Your Cognitive Revolution

How has your thinking about selling changed to the increased sophistication of your customers and their buying processes?
Circle the scale below to show your present position on the scale from left (pre-revolution or out-of-date) to right (post revolution or ideal).

FROM: OLD FOCUS	Circle your present rating:					TO: NEW FOCUS	Page
Focus on Products & Services	●	1	2	3	4	5	● Focus on Solutions & Results	221
Think Features & Benefits	●	1	2	3	4	5	● Think Business Impact/Metrics	250
Think Sales Process	●	1	2	3	4	5	● Think Buying Process	192
Think Buying Decision	●	1	2	3	4	5	● Think Business Decision	204
Think 'What is in it for me?'	●	1	2	3	4	5	● Think 'What is in it for buyer?'	73

Score: _____

The B2B Revolution   Appendix

IV. THE RESULTS YOU GET: Your Revolutionary Pay-back

How has your daily sales approach, or behavior responded to the increased sophistication of your customers and their buying processes? Circle the scale below to show your present position on the scale from left (pre-revolution or out-of-date) to right (post revolution or ideal).

FROM: OLD PAY-BACK		*Circle your present rating:*					TO: NEW PAY-BACK	Page
Buyer Slow To Engage	●	1	2	3	4	5	● Buyer Engages Fully	149
Limited Repeat Business	●	1	2	3	4	5	● Lifetime Customers	299
Limited Referrals	●	1	2	3	4	5	● Endless Referrals	329
Seen As Another Supplier	●	1	2	3	4	5	● Seen As A Strategic Partner	314
Average or Below Win Rates	●	1	2	3	4	5	● Above Average Win Rates	289

Score: _____

CALCULATING YOUR SCORE

> ## CALCULATING YOUR SCORE
> Write in your scores from each page to arrive at the total below.
>
> **I. WHO <u>YOU</u> ARE:** _____
>
> **II. WHAT <u>YOU</u> DO:** _____
>
> **III. HOW <u>YOU</u> THINK:** _____
>
> **IV. THE RESULTS <u>YOU</u> GET:** _____
>
> **YOUR TOTAL SCORE:** _____

If you are leading the charge in terms of revolutionizing how you sell, then your total score would be 110 (22 items with a max of 5 points each). Here is a scale to see just how revolutionary you are:

91-110 — You are the **Che Guevara of Selling** — the poster boy for a new order of selling. You are passionate about change and have put today's more sophisticated buyer at the centre of how you sell.

61-90 — You are the **Chairman Mao of Selling**. Change is coming but there is going to be a long march first. Ensuring that the change in how you sell keeps pace with that in buying is a priority.

41-60 — You are the **Charles Darwin of Selling**. You agree that there has to be change, but it will be an evolution, as opposed to a revolution. You will change but, but will it happen quickly enough? Greater momentum is likely to be required.

Under 40 — You are a **Marie Antoinette of Selling** — 'Let them eat cake!' Except it is let them (as in buyers) read the proposal, let them follow our sales process or let them prequalify in, or out. This strategy could be the end of you!

ABOUT THE AUTHORS

John and Ray are successful salespeople turned sales consultants. They come at selling from a new angle – that of the buyer.

John O'Gorman has been selling and consulting internationally for organisations such as Digital, Compaq and Eontec (acquired by Siebel). He completed his International MBA in 2004 and holds a Bachelor of Commerce degree.

Ray Collis has consulted to companies such as Smith + Nephew, Nilfisk, BT Wholesale and Norsk Hydro. He has Master's and Bachelor's degrees in Business and Marketing.

John and Ray act as sales advisers to ambitious sales organisations, government agencies and educational institutions. Visit their web portal for 1000s of insights, tips and techniques:

www.SellerInsights.com
1000s of Articles & Tips

THE ASG GROUP OF SALES CONSULTANTS

John and Ray established The ASG Group in 2007 – a specialist B2B sales consulting practice helping sales managers to boost sales. The letters ASG stand for Accelerated Sales Growth – the company's methodology for accelerating growth.

The company's ground-breaking research with many of the world's largest companies clearly pinpoints those strategies, skills and techniques most effective at winning the sale. The ASG Group uses this information to help managers to meet specific targets for win rates and sales growth.

In addition, the company's extensive library of best practice in respect of sales and marketing enables managers to benchmark all aspects of sales team performance.

The ASG Group
Sales Consultants
Dublin, Ireland.
www.theASGgroup.com

Lightning Source UK Ltd.
Milton Keynes UK
UKOW05n0151161013

219099UK00001B/82/P